Consumer choice in housing

The beginnings of a house buyer revolt

**Ken Bartlett, Malcolm Potter and Jim Meikle,
Francis Duffy, Ritsuko Ozaki, Julian Hakes,
Raymond Young and Alan Hooper**

The **Joseph Rowntree Foundation** has supported this project as part of its programme of research and innovative development projects, which it hopes will be of value to policy makers, practitioners and service users. The facts presented and views expressed in this report are, however, those of the authors and not necessarily those of the Foundation.

© Joseph Rowntree Foundation 2002

Published for the Joseph Rowntree Foundation by YPS

ISBN 1 84263 065 2

Cover design by Adkins Design

Prepared and printed by:
York Publishing Services Ltd
64 Hallfield Road
Layerthorpe
York
YO31 7ZQ
Tel: 01904 430033 Fax: 01904 430868 E-mail: orders@yps.ymn.co.uk

CONTENTS

Notes on the Contributors

Ken Bartlett   Ken Bartlett is an adviser to the Joseph Rowntree Foundation and directs the Rethinking Housebuilding research programme.

Malcolm Potter   Malcolm Potter is an architect with many years of housing experience and is now a senior consultant with Davis Langdon Consultancy.

Jim Meikle   Jim Meikle is a Partner of Davis Langdon Consultancy and has a particular interest in international building stock and construction statistics.

Francis Duffy   Francis Duffy is an architect and writer, specialising in the design of working environments. He is one of the founders of DEGW, an international architectural practice, and is a past President of the RIBA (Royal Institute of British Architects) and the Architects' Council of Europe.

Ritsuko Ozaki   Ritsuko Ozaki is a Research Fellow at SPRU (Science and Technology Policy Research), University of Sussex. Her background is sociology.

Julian Hakes   Julian Hakes is Director of Hakes Associates Architects and tutors at the University of Cambridge Department of Architecture.

Raymond Young   Raymond Young is an Honorary Senior Research Fellow at the Department of Urban Studies at the University of Glasgow.

Alan Hooper   Alan Hooper is Professor of Housing and Planning in the Department of City and Regional Planning, Cardiff University.

INTRODUCTION: SUPPLIERS AND CUSTOMERS IN UK HOUSING – LEAPING OVER THE GAP

Ken Bartlett

Since the industrial revolution, and arguably earlier, decisions on the provision of housing in the UK have been dominated by suppliers, not by those who live in houses. Francis Duffy, in his contribution to this book, records the 'colossal and monolithic certainty' of young architects 30 years ago that 'British society knew what sort of housing people ought to have'. Even as recently as four years ago, the chairman of a small house-building company could report with satisfaction to shareholders that the company had reduced its range of house types: 'we now sell what we wish to sell, not what our customers wish us to sell'!

Over the last three years, the climate has fundamentally changed. A number of factors have contributed:

1   the rise in Britain of a consumer culture, which regards choice in everything as a natural right

2   growing dissatisfaction with the standards of building – the image of the house-building industry is very poor and the public is increasingly aware

3   concern in the industry itself about its future.

Over the last five years, the production of new houses in the UK has fallen by over 25 per cent – from 200,000 to under 140,000 – the lowest peacetime total since 1924. Significantly, influential voices within the industry now recognise that the problem – and its solution – is related to public image, customer perception and customer satisfaction. The Housing Forum's new Customer Satisfaction Survey is now available on the web, bringing the same level of scrutiny to new houses as to new cars. Sir Michael Latham, author of the Latham report and chairman of Wilmott Dixon, in an address to the Greater Peterborough Chamber of Commerce training and enterprise seminar (February 2001), said:

> There is a gap. It must be bridged. The issue for the industry is whether that bridge is to be a robust Tower Bridge or a flimsy pontoon. The building of that bridge needs to begin yesterday. Clients are no longer prepared to wait … they will increasingly take matters into their own hands by choosing out of area or even overseas firms which will perform more to their satisfaction.

Latham's gap is the context and policy relevance of these essays. They underline the key issue, but they also provide ideas for the future, aimed at enabling the house-building industry in the UK to leap over the gap and double or triple its output. An increase in new housing provision is an urgent national priority, because many existing houses are very poor quality, unsustainable in energy terms, in bad environments and poorly located in relation to essential services. We need to replace existing houses as well as providing for new households. However, the house-building industry does not currently command sufficient confidence with consumers to allow it to expand. If the industry is to expand, it must rebrand itself by responding to the growing demand for consumer choice. These essays aim to identify the characteristics of new houses that would attract consumers. Together, they constitute an analysis of the gap between housing providers and consumers. They also offer positive suggestions about how the gap can be closed.

In the first chapter, Malcolm Potter and Jim Meikle of Davis Langdon reflect on the hundred-year inheritance of UK housing. They conclude that future generations have an ageing housing stock and an ageing population, divided in its ability to pay for the future. Fiscal policies have exacerbated the problem by discriminating against certain social or economic groups and causing division/exclusion:

> ... the provision of personal subsidies in the UK (housing benefit) has led to rent increases that only reinforce the disadvantages of low-income households and limit their access to good housing. Similarly, policies that place no limits on capital gains from home-ownership ultimately increase the divide between the wealthy and the poor, making access to the sector increasingly difficult for those on low incomes.

Potter and Meikle's discussion covers a range of EU countries, giving a backdrop to housing provision across Western Europe that gives a clue to how questions of customer choice may be influenced.

Francis Duffy, architect and founder of DEGW, is an acknowledged leader in the field of workplace design. He starts by recalling attitudes towards housing in the architectural profession at the beginning of his career:

I helped to prepare a document for architects on house types called *Generic Plans*. I now realise that this was an exercise in variety reduction ... the big priority was to reduce choice for users rather than to open up options. It was not obvious to me at the time that this kind of idea was far more likely to appeal to the construction industry than to those on the demand side of the supply/demand equation.

Duffy comments that attitudes were very similar 'in the capitalist United States and in welfare state Britain as much as in the post-Stalinist East'. He characterises the last 30 years in both office design and housing as the story of a long slow but cumulatively huge retreat from such monolithic attitudes: from top down to bottom up; from central control to delegated authority; from variety reduction to the acceptance of diversity. Duffy then discusses changing attitudes which relate to shifts in societal priorities: from the long to the short term; from fixed conventions to increasing fluidity in the use of time and space; from imposed to negotiated order.

Ritsuko Ozaki of the Science and Technology Policy Research Unit, Sussex University, concentrates on the gap between what people expect and what they are offered. Customer satisfaction is a key driver for the UK house-building industry, but the shift from producer convenience to customer focus is difficult and uncomfortable. Even so, analysing the gap between customer aspirations and what has been delivered enables builders to improve performance. Dr Ozaki examines this gap in detail in three main areas: workmanship, service provision and house design. Her emphasis is on the way customer-focused performance can improve business and the way Japanese house builders have used careful analysis of customer wishes to promote their business. Significantly, she comments that while

'UK house builders do not offer as much flexibility in house design as their Japanese counterparts ... the UK house buyers have more specific ideas about their homes'.

The fourth essay by Julian Hakes of Hakes Associates Architects and Designers seeks to understand what it is about older properties that gives them their enduring attraction. He believes that the appeal of old houses resides primarily in the quality of experience that they provide and goes on to describe a drift away in modern building from the intuitive relationship between the person and the environment. He draws attention to the special affinity we seem to have for the natural 'real' materials of old buildings, like stone and wood. By contrast, the typical new house is a place where surfaces may look like stone or wood, but lack their feel and smell. We do not have to accept desensitised environments; natural materials are not necessarily expensive or requiring of specialist skills. On the continent, they have been formed into products suited to the modern construction industry. Humanness and lifestyle should guide the production and design of our houses. 'We respond to light and shade, to our acoustic environment, to enclosure and exposure, to the quality of the air that we breathe.' A good house will therefore address both these unchanging human attributes and culturally conditioned lifestyle choices. People like space that is flexible but not neutral or impersonal and materials with which they have an affinity.

Raymond Young, an honorary senior research fellow at Glasgow University's Urban Studies department, writes about the position of individual house buyers faced with the need to choose a home. It is an intimidating prospect – a huge investment. People have fears about building quality and the possibility of being conned, and there is a feeling on the part of buyers that they do not know much about modern design or issues like sustainability. The key point made by Young is the need to create an intelligent client, not just a consumer of a product. He draws attention to an information vacuum. In computers and car construction, for example, a range of independently published magazines analyse construction and cost, and give information on choice; there is no such equivalent in housing. Television programmes are common but largely concentrate on questions of interior fashion. In Scandinavia (and Japan), people are able to visit house exhibitions where they can see affordable homes where the method of construction is proudly demonstrated. By contrast, in the UK, most exhibit show houses are top of the range and not generally affordable, and there is no emphasis on construction methods. Yet, the 100-house 'Homes of the Future' development, part of Glasgow City of Architecture and Design 1999, exhibited houses which then sold extremely quickly as high-density housing. This example is particularly relevant in the context of the UK consensus that we need to build high-quality, high-density homes in inner urban areas. If this policy is to succeed, the general public – and potential residents in particular – have to be given opportunities to inspect high-density developments, to learn in detail about their construction and to be able to form a direct assessment of the quality of life on offer. Only in this way will it be possible for house building in the future to test itself against consumer aspirations and to build up public confidence.

In the final contribution, Alan Hooper, Professor of Housing and Planning at Cardiff University, reflects on how consumer choice in housing is conditioned not only by the quality of a dwelling, but also by other sets of institutions and structures which constitute the market in any given context. Is there, for example, anything intrinsically desirable about owner-occupation, or is the fact that ownership is the majority choice in the UK based not on the intrinsic desirability of ownership in itself, but on the desirability conferred on it by circumstances? Thus, in the UK, housing market dynamics, land regulation and tax policies have structured residential options so that housing choices are constrained. These factors have led to ownership becoming the dominant form of tenure at 67 per cent nationally (1991 Census). The domination of ownership has now become such a fact of life that it is easy to forget that, in 1969, less than half of UK householders were owners (46 per cent). Hooper observes that, despite this, little is known in depth about the housing preferences of owner-occupiers in general and the occupants of new housing in particular, although some trends and contradictions have become apparent. For example, consumers want more space, but rising costs and the indirect effects of planning are actually reducing space in the dwellings. Innovation in the construction process makes individual options possible, but so far the introduction of any real flexibility in individual design or layout has been negligible.

The views of consumers used to be an optional extra, at best a matter of polite interest. They are now vital to the house-building industry's future and survival. The expansion of flexibility and choice, and with it the rate at which the UK housing stock is renewed, must become a joint agenda for the industry, and for all those who determine and regulate their working environment. The common denominator of these essays is that the involvement of consumers making choice is no longer an optional extra or a regrettable inconvenience; it is the very engine of change.

1 HOMES FOR TODAY AND TOMORROW – A COMPARATIVE REVIEW IN THE EUROPEAN CONTEXT

Malcolm Potter and Jim Meikle

Summary

A recent report on European housing concluded that 'the routes to good housing differ sharply and levels and varieties of support vary greatly' (*Housing Policy in the EU Member States*, working document 14). It is worth considering why there is such diversity and how the different approaches to housing provision impact on choice. This chapter draws on data and views of housing provision from a variety of sources. Because it does so, it highlights in places the dearth of reliable comparative data on this important topic. The authors have been selective in the data and views used and, where appropriate, have commented on them. It is important not to overlook the fact that such data can, of course, conceal large internal variations.

Questions of choice

At the broadest level, housing choice is affected by a number of factors:

- the existing supply, type and quality of housing

- changes in demographic and socio-economic patterns

- the nature of tenure and how this is administered

- accessibility, quality, affordability and the mechanisms for support.

Each of these is a major topic in its own right and cannot be dealt with in detail in this brief review. What is done here is to raise questions through an examination of the principal characteristics of contemporary housing and to show, by highlighting common issues and differences, how choice can be affected, particularly for the poorer sections of society. If these examples succeed only in provoking thought, this chapter has served its purpose.

Examples and comments focus primarily on a limited number of countries but reference is made to all EU member states where this is particularly relevant. As indicated above, obtaining useful and consistent data on housing in Europe has proved difficult and highlights the need for reliable data that address the key issues for policy makers.

The overall context

The average annual rate of growth in the population of Western Europe over the past 20 years has been in the order of 0.28 per cent (5.6 per cent over the 20-year period). Although this rate has generally been consistent across most countries, there have been marked variations. Particular exceptions include Luxembourg and Holland where growth has been as high as 1.0 per cent and 0.5 per cent respectively and Portugal and Italy where growth has been 0.01 per cent or less. By comparison, the average annual population growth rate of the United States was 1.08 per cent over a similar period.

Projections for the next 20 years generally indicate that the rate of growth is likely to slow down to an annual average of 0.1 per cent. France, Holland and the UK are expected to exceed this figure while populations in Spain and Germany are forecast to fall, the latter by as much as 4 per cent over the 20-year period (Figure 1.1). It is understood that the population growth trends generally assume no significant change in current migration rates.

Figure 1.1 Population (in thousands) in the European Union, 1980–2020

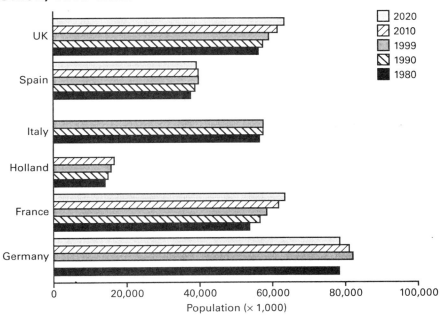

Note: There are no comparable data for Italy for 2010 and 2020; Holland for 2020; and Germany for 1990.

These projections incorporate two important features:

- an ageing population

- reductions in average household size.

An average rise of 4 per cent in the over-65 population in the European Union over the past 20 years implies that the birth rate in most countries is declining (Figure 1.2). This is borne out by the forecast that the under-25 population is expected to fall, in some case by as much as 7 per cent (Figure 1.3).

The picture is further altering as a result of decreasing average household sizes and corresponding increases in demand for one- and two-person accommodation (Figure 1.4). The implications of these changes is important as they exacerbate existing problems of matching housing demand with suitable supply.

Figure 1.2 Percentage of the European Union population over the age of 65, 1999, 2020

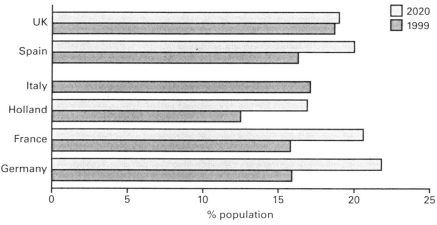

Note: There are no comparable data for Italy for 2020.

Figure 1.3 Percentage of the European Union population under the age of 25, 1999, 2020

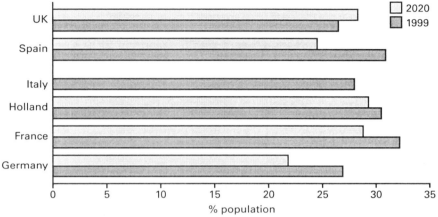

Note: There are no comparable data for Italy for 2020.

Figure 1.4 Percentage distribution of one- and two-person households in the European Union, 1980, 1999

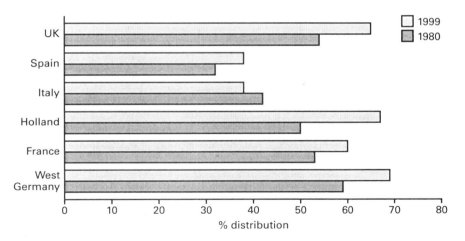

Population densities can impact on the quality of day-to-day living and vary considerably from one European country to another. Holland and Belgium top the league for the highest average densities – they are three times more densely populated than France; not far behind are the UK and Germany – more than twice as densely populated as France. The continuing trend of migration of people away from the countryside to large towns in most countries adds to the special problems associated with high-density urban living. Regional differences, such as those that distinguish the North and South of England and a similar divide in Italy, are also common in many other European countries and further impact on the factors that influence the nature and quality of housing provision. Western European urbanisation levels range from 58 per cent (Finland) to 99.8 per cent (Belgium).

Housing stock

Table 1.1 provides a broad snapshot of the housing stock of the principal European countries in the early 1990s. This shows considerable variation in overall scale and in supply conditions. Despite this, average dwelling occupancy lies within a relatively narrow band (though averages themselves can conceal more than they reveal). Variations in average dwelling occupancy probably reflect vacancy rates and the prevalence of second homes. Levels of urbanisation show some relatively marked contrasts.

The figures in Table 1.1 suggest that the rate of new building is uniformly relatively low (generally less than 1 per cent per annum, implying a crude replacement period of more than 100 years). In addition, only a small proportion of housing investment involves the replacement of existing stock – most new housing is built to satisfy increased household formation and second homes. New housing is also necessary to cope with regional shifts in population. The consequence of regular low levels of

Table 1.1 Dwelling stock in the principal European countries in the early 1990s

	East Germany	West Germany	France	Holland	Italy	Spain	UK
Dwelling stock (000s) 1998/99	7,017	26,839	26,237	5,892	23,232	17,154	23,622
Average occupancy	2.29	2.36	2.16	2.6	2.5	2.27	2.45
Stock per 1,000 inhabitants	480	445	490	414		481	417
Losses from stock (as % of stock)	0.78	0.05	0.28	0.19	0.21	0.72	0.07
New dwelling completions (% of stock)	0.89	0.96	1.18	1.64	1.20	1.60	0.83
Net gains % of stock	**0.11**	**0.91**	**0.90**	**1.45**	**0.99**	**0.88**	**0.76**
Gross investment in dwellings (% of gross capital formation)	35		25	27	28	21	20
Level of urbanisation (%)	87		75	61	67	76	89
Dwelling stock built pre 1945 (% of stock)	na	33	43	28	30	27	50

Source: Netherlands Ministry of Housing and Physical Planning and Environment, 1992.

investment is that most countries have a high and increasing proportion of older stock, much of which was built before 1945 – UK heads the category for longevity. In recent years, in the UK, demolition has included a growing proportion of stock built since 1945 – a factor that compounds the problems of ageing stock.

The rate of house building has declined over the last 20 years – the number of newly completed dwellings for the whole of the EU fell by over 16 per cent between 1980 and 1995. However, overall capital spending on housing construction over the same period fell by only 10 per cent suggesting increased investment in refurbishment and repair of existing stock. With a few notable exceptions, where new house building has increased (Spain, Ireland and Portugal), recent trends are characterised by a slowing down or declining supply of new housing in most EU countries.

Tenure

While a broad overview of housing provision and demographic trends is helpful in understanding the 'big picture', it is essential to look more closely at the way in which housing is provided in different parts of Europe and how this in turn affects an individual's access to housing.

At the end of the nineteenth century, the prevalence of widespread poverty and inadequate housing in Western Europe led to a review of legislation and health standards. Programmes of demolition and new housing were established to replace slum housing, particularly in urban areas. In order to make the new improved housing fully accessible to all members of the community, a range of measures was introduced to ensure that traditional market mechanisms did not exclude those it was targeted to assist. This gave rise to a variety of not-for-profit housing providers ranging from national and local government to privately sponsored landlords. By the late 1920s, rented accommodation, at below market rates, had become widespread and was almost universal throughout Western Europe after the Second World War. Although this represented only a relatively small proportion of the total housing stock, it was the beginning of a significant change that was to gain momentum.

Policies aimed at relaxing rental control were introduced as a response to the perception that rent restrictions were causing reduced accessibility and under-investment in repair and maintenance, and were first apparent in Northern and Western Europe during the 1960s. By the second half of the 1980s, compulsory rent controls had largely been abandoned.

Analysis of current housing stock by tenure clearly reflects the variety of housing policies adopted by different European countries (Figures 1.5 and 1.6). They may be grouped into four categories:[1]

1   Those with the largest social rented sector where government made relatively high investments in housing – this group includes Holland, Sweden and the UK.

2   Those with a lower proportion of social rented housing combined with a sizeable private rented sector that has been subject to less restrictive rent controls and larger owner-occupied sectors.

3   Those with large owner-occupied sectors and relatively small social rented sectors where government investment was small. This group includes Ireland, Italy, Belgium and Luxembourg.

4   Those with large owner-occupied sectors, minimal rented sectors and (until recently) declining low quality private rented sectors. This group includes Portugal, Spain and Greece.

Figure 1.5 Percentage of social and private rented properties of total rented in Europe (early 1980s)

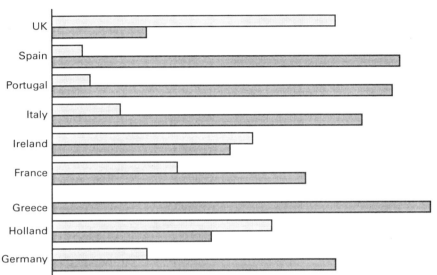

Overall, owner-occupation has steadily increased throughout the twentieth century and is now the largest tenure accounting for 56 per cent of all housing in the European Union. Increases have been particularly noticeable in those countries where government investment in social housing has traditionally been greatest, such as Holland and the UK. Owner-occupation in the UK, for example, has increased by nearly 15 per cent since 1980, primarily because of Right to Buy transfers from the public rented sector to the private owner-occupied.

**Figure 1.6 Percentage of rented and owner-occupied
properties in different European countries (early 1980s)**

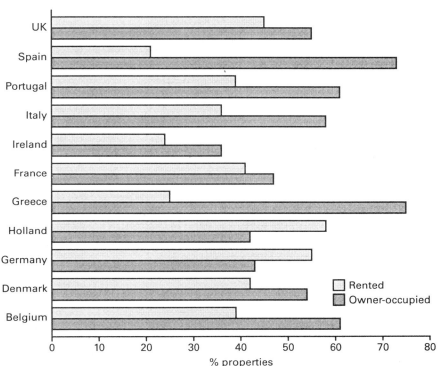

Quality

Definitions of quality among the types of tenure tend to be crude
and to focus on simple measures, such as levels of occupation,
lack of amenity, space per person, number of bed spaces and
usable space. Different measures give different answers and take
little or no account of important considerations such as location,
levels of poverty, crime, anti-social behaviour, management
support, accessibility for the disabled and elderly, all of which
contribute to our ultimate sense of well-being towards the place
in which we live.

Some general observations on quality can be drawn from the data:

- With some exceptions, notably the UK, the number of rooms in newly built dwellings is reducing.

- Usable space in newly built dwellings is increasing.

- Overall, occupation levels in the rented sector (social and private) tend to be lower than for owner-occupied dwellings.

Reductions in dwelling sizes are to be expected and are broadly consistent with current population trends, as are the general lower occupation levels in the rented sector. Increased provision of usable space is to be welcomed but this is by no means consistently the case.

Attempts to develop more useful assessments of quality draw together a range of quality measures[2] to arrive at a more comprehensive picture of current housing standards. The recently introduced Housing Quality Indicators (UK) adopt this approach. Another example is the Quality Index.[3] This offers an overall rating of quality based on a variety of indicators. These ratings resulted in the following general conclusions:

- Individual housing space and privacy are lower in Ireland, Portugal, Spain, Greece, Italy and Austria, and most generous in Luxembourg, Holland, Sweden and the UK.

- Single-family dwellings are most prevalent in Ireland and the UK, and least prevalent in Greece, Germany and Italy.

- The countries with the largest proportion of pre-1918 dwellings are Finland, Sweden, Spain, Italy, Holland and the UK.

- The Scandinavian countries, Germany, UK and Holland have the highest amenity levels as defined by the standard measures relating to the provision of basic facilities.

- Overall, the quality of housing provision in Europe is improving but still varies considerably from region to region.

Despite the generally reassuring nature of these conclusions, it is all too apparent that a large proportion of the people in Europe live in conditions that are far from satisfactory when judged by today's standards. Because measures of amenity provide an incomplete picture, more detailed statistics are required to form a fuller assessment of housing quality.

Accessibility and affordability

The need to provide housing that is affordable has been the main driver behind the housing policies pursued by European governments since the early twentieth century. These have focused on various combinations of control and subsidy relating to rent, capital investment and the individual. Table 1.2 shows the principal subsidy systems in operation at the end of the twentieth century.

The principal measures to promote affordability can best be reviewed under the different forms of housing tenure.

Owner-occupation

Support for this sector has relied primarily on tax relief on mortgage payments and targeted support for particular categories

Table 1.2 Subsidy systems in operation in different European countries, 1992

	Capital subsidy newly built		Capital subsidy improvement		Rent allowance subsidies	
	Rental dwellings	Owner-occupied dwellings	Rental dwellings	Owner-occupied dwellings	Occupant rental dwellings	Occupant owner-occupied dwellings
Belgium	X	X	X	X	X	X
Denmark	X	–	X	X	X	–
West Germany	X	X	X	X	X	X
East Germany	X	X	X	X	X	X
Holland	X	X	X	X	X	X
Greece	–	X	–	X	X	X
France	X	X	X	X	X	X
Ireland	–	X	–	–	–	–
Italy	X	X	X	X	X	–
Luxembourg	–	X	–	–	–	–
Portugal	X	X	X	X	X	–
Spain	X	X	X	X	X	–
United Kingdom	X	–	X	X	X	X

X = Yes, exists; – = No, doesn't exist.

Source: Netherlands Ministry of Housing and Physical Planning and Environment 1992.

such as first-time buyers. Typical problems associated with this sector include:

- mortgage arrears and repossession

- changes in family circumstances through separation and divorce creating demands for short-term rental accommodation

- poor maintenance by low-income owners, particularly the elderly

- lack of facilities for the elderly.

Private rented sector

This sector still provides housing for about one-fifth of the EU's population. With a few notable exceptions, such as Germany, the private rented sector has been less well supported than others. There have been indications of a revival in the last ten years as rent controls are being relaxed in some countries. Typical problems associated with this sector include:

- poor households unable to afford owner-occupation and without access to social rented housing

- ageing, low-income households in poor accommodation

- young, low income, living singly and collectively in poor accommodation.

Figure 1.7 Owner-occupation and social rented accommodation as a percentage of total stock

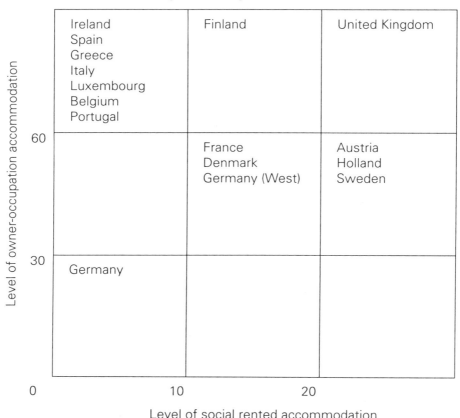

Level of social rented accommodation

Social rented sector

This sector also provides housing for about one-fifth of EU households. Landlords are mainly housing associations and co-operatives, with the particular exceptions of Austria, UK and Ireland where local authorities have responsibility for the majority of social housing provision. With the exception of Ireland and Germany, this sector has been in decline since the mid-1980s. Social rented housing in some countries has acquired a poor reputation – the choice of last resort.

Typical problems associated with this sector include:

- reductions in the overall quality of the stock, resulting from policies encouraging home-ownership

- poor maintenance and management arising from reduced investment

- ageing, low-income households

- poor households unable to afford owner-occupation

- high turnover of tenants and increasing incidence of anti-social behaviour (particularly in inner cities).

Reflection on the way forward

Problems associated with affordability and access to good housing are not exclusive to any one type of tenure – examples of unacceptable housing conditions can be found in all three of the broad groups considered here. Low income levels and problems associated with the elderly and disabled pose similar difficulties for all countries; however, they may be exacerbated by policies that have the effect of discriminating against certain social or economic groups. For example, the provision of personal subsidies in the UK (Housing Benefit) has led to rent increases that only reinforce the disadvantages of low-income households and limit access to good housing. Similarly, policies that place no limits on capital gains from home-ownership ultimately increase the divide between the wealthy and the poor, making access to that sector increasingly difficult for those on low incomes.

The rise of homelessness is the recent phenomenon common to most European countries and is not exclusive to areas of high urbanisation. Homelessness has become a matter of major concern to those responsible for housing policy. It reflects a fundamental malaise across all housing tenures and in particular is seen as an indicator of the increasing barriers to affordable housing. The causes of homelessness are well documented but in summary are broadly attributed to:

- rising immigration

- growing incidence in family breakdown

- rising unemployment especially among the young

- inadequate social security and welfare systems

- lack of community care and health facilities.

What this list highlights is not so much shortcomings in the provision of housing but a much wider set of issues that together make for healthy communities. A great deal of past investment has been aimed at providing the physical environment – improving facilities and amenities – the bricks and mortar of housing provision. Although good housing should be based on adequate and up-to-date facilities and standards, it is increasingly recognised that local and national well-being and prosperity depend upon the successful integration of a number of other factors. These include employment, health and education provision, social and economic variety, and involvement in the local community. For the past ten years or more, a number of countries have started to develop practical solutions that take account of these broader themes but the task is fraught with problems. Creating economic opportunities is difficult where employment opportunities are few, especially where engineering social change is dependent on attracting a variety of tenures and socio-economic groups.

Increasing pressure on the use of inner city land, infrastructure and transport not only creates problems but also stimulates innovation. Growing concern for sustainable development in its widest sense is adding momentum to the search for new and better solutions. Regeneration takes time and conscious planning but there are already sufficient signs of success to suggest that this is possible and better living conditions could be available to a greater proportion of society. However, if this is to happen, changing patterns of living – increased time spent in the home, longer life expectancy with, possibly, decreasing mobility and changes in household size over time all have to be taken into account. So, too, have the lessons of the past hundred years which have left future generations with an ageing housing stock and an ageing population divided in its ability to pay for the future.

Notes

The principal source of data is 'Housing Statistics in the European Union 2000', compiled by the Research Institute for Housing, Urban and Mobility Studies, Delft University of Technology, The Netherlands, 2000 – except where otherwise stated.

1   Categories as classified in *Housing Policy in EU Member States*, Working Document 14. The document is available from The Directorate General for Research, Working Document, Social Affairs series, W14, European Parliament 12/96 (www.europarl.eu.int/workingpaper/soci/w14/default_en.htm)

2   Persons per room, space per person, single family, percentage of dwellings pre-1918, units without bath/shower, proportion of 'good' units and central heating.

3   See *Housing Policy in EU Member States,* Working Document 14 (details in note 1 above).

2 Changing lifestyles and aspirations: designing for contemporary customers

Francis Duffy

Summary

This chapter takes an external and very personal view of user involvement in housing. A backward glance over the last 40 years is the basis for some speculations about the possible future of housing both as a building type and as a design and delivery process. However, the chief method of enquiry is to compare the impact of consumers on housing with what appears to be the far larger and more direct recent impact of user involvement on office design and office tenure. This comparative approach allows the following questions to be addressed:

- Are consumerist pressures stronger in housing or offices?

- Will consumer pressures make housing more like offices or offices more like housing?

- Or will both building types continue to be as separate and distinct as they are today?

Continued overleaf ...

Three main conclusions are drawn. The first is that, although in recent years consumerist pressures have been more visible and effective in shaping office buildings and interiors than housing, recent trends in office design seem likely in the longer term to make office buildings much less distinctive as a building type. Some office buildings may become more like housing. Some may even merge with housing. The second conclusion is that consumerist trends give us reason to expect that much existing practice in design process, delivery and tenure in both housing and offices is unsatisfactory and is likely to become increasingly unpopular. Hence, the third conclusion: the possibility exists today, as never before, for far more creative synergy between the design and delivery of housing and offices.

Method

This chapter is written not by a historian, nor by a sociologist, nor by someone who knows the field of housing design particularly well. It is written by an architect whose life in practice has been very largely spent in what is generally thought to be a totally different field, workplace design. My only advantage as a commentator on housing is a different perspective derived from:

- contact with some very interesting, demanding and rapidly changing clients

- international experience, especially of cultural differences within allegedly homogeneous, global businesses

- a strong interest in and extensive experience of large-scale user participation in the design of offices

- an equally strong interest in the impact of user involvement in office design at all scales from individual workplaces to the shaping of the urban fabric

- consequential strong feelings about the need for architects to respond to rising user expectations of the working environment despite the supply-led attitudes of large parts of the construction and property industries.

The method I have adopted, if it can be called a method in any formal sense, is comparative. I have attempted to use my own experience of international developments in user involvement in office design over 40 years to throw some light on what seem in some ways to be parallel, but in other ways very different, trends and developments in consumers' experience of the design of UK housing.

Housing in the 1960s

It is not entirely true to say that I have no experience of housing design. Recently, my colleagues in DEGW have been involved in the development for DETR of Housing Quality Indicators – an exercise that sprang out of our evaluative work in office design. Moreover, my own professional career began in the early 1960s not in office design but in social housing. This was very much the fashion for socially committed young architects at the time.

What astonishes me today, looking back at the work we did then, was, first, our colossal and monolithic certainty as young architects that we knew what we were doing – which was certainly not the case – and, second, our equally solid confidence that British society knew what sort of housing people ought to have. In retrospect, the latter assumption seems to me to be by far the more extraordinary. The highly influential Parker Morris Report, for example, was published about that time. It seemed to us to be a kind of bible, promulgating standards for public housing with such confidence that little or no possibility of deviation from a sociologically established norm was necessary or even possible. The word 'consumer' was not exactly on everyone's lips in the architectural circles in which I moved. Nor, astonishingly, did it occur to us that change might reasonably be anticipated in housing needs.

In my work at the National Building Agency in 1965/66, I helped to prepare a document for architects on house types called *Generic Plans.* I now realise that this was an exercise in variety reduction. The document was imbued with implicit notion that the big priority was to reduce choice for users rather than to open up options. It was not obvious to me at the time that this kind of idea was far more likely to appeal to the construction industry than to those on the demand side of the supply/demand equation in housing.

The parallel with office design

In the mid-1960s, very similar attitudes were prevalent in office design – in the capitalist United States and in welfare state Britain as much as in the post-Stalinist East. Architects knew best, of course. Well above them in the decision-making hierarchy of big business, corporate clients knew even better. *They* knew exactly how much and what kind of office space workers should be given. Manuals laying down precise standards for the allocation of office space and office furniture rained down, as it were, out of the sky, as edicts from the headquarters of international corporations in New York or Chicago or Detroit. These standards were all but immutable. They were designed to be applied without question everywhere in the world – regardless of cultural, social, economic or even ergonomic circumstances. Similar attitudes existed in the public sector. In the old Property Services Agency (PSA), for example, then the government department responsible for all British civil service office accommodation, the allocation of office space at every level in the hierarchy was all sewn up. The same centralising and hierarchically controlled assumptions linger to this day in PSA's US equivalent, the Federal General Services Administration (GSA).

The correlation between the physical arrangements of the office and the dominant value system of society at that time is easily demonstrated. What seems to have mattered most in post-Second World War society was order – not negotiated order but a quasi-military order imposed from above. Hierarchy, inevitably, was also important at a period in which many careers in many organisations were expected to last for 40 years. People traded freedom for security. Each step in each extended career was carefully marked as a major event in physical terms – by the allocation of more space, more windows, more carpet. Once discipline and hierarchy had been established, the next most valued feature of this kind of society, as reflected in its office accommodation, seems to have been the elimination of individual choice. There were undoubtedly economic reasons for the homogenisation of office space but a powerful cultural message was also transmitted every minute of every day to everyone who occupied such rigorously impersonal offices. As the Japanese proverb says, 'It is the nail that stands out that gets hammered down'.

Changing values

Two kinds of parallel have now emerged: first the possible parallels – or differences – between two building types, housing and offices, and, second, the parallels between the physical form of each of these building types and the collective values of society at the time that each new wave of building is created. The past is indeed another country. It is abundantly clear that we live in a very different society in the UK today from that of the Britain of 40 years ago. The last four decades can be regarded very crudely as the story of a long, slow but cumulatively huge retreat from the monolithic attitudes sketched above. If this is so, there may be many similarities in the development of both housing and offices that would reflect the same underlying but consistent trends in the evolution of our society and our culture.

But are the trends really consistent in both housing and office design?

In office design, it has become usual to summarise major long-term trends in roughly the following way. Decisions about the form of offices are being affected by decision-making processes that are shifting from being predominantly:

- top down to bottom up

- centrally controlled to delegating authority and empowering people

- focused on variety reduction to becoming far more tolerant of diversity.

These changes in the procurement process for offices have a lot to do with such major shifts in technological and business priorities as from:

- centralised to networked office technologies

- emphasising the long-term planning to short-term responsiveness

- local protectionism to global competition

- rigid conventions in the use of space and time to increasing acceptance of fluidity

- imposed order to 'anything goes'.

These changes have been stimulated by the increasing economic importance of office work in the modern economy. In the last two decades, information technology has been a particularly powerful agent of change. The demography of the office workforce is also changing, in some sectors more rapidly than others, as knowledge work replaces clerical processes. Hence, it is hardly surprising that the last five years have been a period of extraordinary movement and experimentation in office design.

A similar potential for significant change exists in housing design for many of the same underlying reasons. Demographic shifts, new patterns of household formation, more disposable income, all-pervasive information technology, new lifestyles, all of these factors lead one to expect a similar explosion of design invention. However, admittedly as an outsider to the field of housing design, I do not sense the same inventive energy, nor do I have the impression that similar changes are under way. Why should this be so?

Differences between housing and offices

The most obvious and architecturally significant difference between housing and offices is that business organisations are often larger, sometimes much larger, than the families, the individuals, the partners who occupy houses and flats. Typically, office buildings are inhabited by far more integrated and complex sociological entities. As office organisations have grown over the decades, aggregations of many individual office workers have tended to produce very large, quite specialised, highly integrated office buildings, with large-scale territorial patterns of space ownership, reflecting complex processes and highly elaborated departmental and individual power structures. In comparison, occupancy patterns in housing produce many, relatively small, units of space that are inherently far more separate and hermetic than workplaces. Hence, the close grain of the architecture of the high-rise apartment block or the suburban tract compared with the generally more open and undifferentiated texture of office space.

Because office organisations are by definition far more 'organised' and coherent than housing collectives, whether in the private and the public sector, they are far more susceptible to consumer pressure. The best example of the impact that organised users can have upon office design is in the way in which democratically established workers' councils effectively banished the open plan in Germany, Scandinavia and The Netherlands from the early 1970s until the late 1990s. What workers said they wanted was individual office rooms for everybody. Office buildings, narrow and specialised enough to accommodate individual office rooms with individual environmental control, are what Northern European office workers got. The whole landscape of office design changed accordingly. But, even without statutory bolstering of user opinion provided by formal workers' council procedures, consumer pressure, especially when labour markets have been tight, has had a profound impact in recent years in pushing up the quality, the safety, the sustainability, the accessibility and the amenity of the working environment. This is true even in the Dilbert-haunted offices of the US.

A critically important difference between housing and offices is tenure. In the UK, most people buy houses. Most enterprises rent office space. Interestingly, in Germany, the opposite tends to be the case. This means that office design in the UK has long been dominated by an institutionally funded system of speculative building by developers who act as intermediaries between tenants and institutional funders.

The consequence has been a severe attenuation of communication between end users and the providers of office space. Office tenants' decision-making timescales have always been far shorter than landlords' – a tendency that has become even more noticeable in recent years as the time horizons for managerial decision making have become ever closer, ever more urgent.

To some extent, this communication gap has been resolved by the increasing professionalism first of property managers and later of facilities managers. However, the existence of these two relatively new professions has also had the effect of adding yet another level of intermediation. Yet another layer now exists between the end users, the individuals, the teams and the departments, who constitute the demand side of the office space equation, and the supply chain, the people who are responsible for constructing and delivering office space. In fact, so strong have in-house service departments become, even in small office organisations, that end users in some organisations have experienced a diminishing say in determining the quality of the office accommodation they occupy. It may even be argued that the behaviour of the in-house property and facilities specialists makes them indistinguishable from and, in effect, part of the supply chain.

Convergence between housing and office design

Given these apparent differences in both the hardware and the software – between the design and the management – of housing and office space it might be assumed that there is very little in common between the two building types.

The differences may be diminishing. For many decades, in office design, a one-to-one ratio between individual office-workers and the workplaces they occupy has been taken for granted. Today, in an increasingly mobile and interactive working environment, this long-standing relationship is weakening. Although very large office buildings continue to be constructed to contain very large organisations, information technology has now introduced the possibility of workplaces being much more dispersed. Indeed, as networking grows in importance, it could be argued that the spatial distribution of office work is reverting to a more domestic form.

In other words, the trends outlined in the section on 'Changing values' above may be encouraging a convergence between what have been for decades two distinct building types. In a couple of decades some, at least, of the sharp contemporary differences between the UK's housing and office stock described above may have begun to disappear.

Two contemporary phenomena help to make this point:

- the increasing frequency of the conversion of obsolete office buildings in city centres into flats

- the growth of home working made possible by robust and portable information technology.

In other words, office buildings are becoming very closely related to apartments and many homes are becoming integrated with increasingly networked office organisations. Perhaps this ought not to be such a surprise. The fabric of seventeenth-century London was much more integrated in terms of occupancy and use than the much more specialised type of urban fabric to which we have now become accustomed. The Inns of Court today continue to be a fascinating example of diversity of use, office work, living and teaching, coexisting with apparent ease within a single urban form.

Comparative trends in consumer demand

Several process-related features are becoming increasingly common in the procurement and delivery of both office and housing design. These features are all indicative of burgeoning consumer power. Each one introduces complexity, uncertainty and possibly risk into what were once three very different but relatively simple delivery procedures – straightforward office buildings largely provided by developers, straightforward public housing provided by well organised local authorities, private housing provided en masse for willing buyers by house builders.

- The involvement of large numbers of users in the design process. While the politics of office organisation are such that it is inherently easier to involve users in design in a relatively disciplined and coherent way, similar techniques of user involvement (focus groups, surveys, gaming) are increasingly used in the housing field.

- The increase in the range of choice available to consumers. Diversity of design options is the principal consequence of pressure from different constituencies that are made up, both in office and housing design, of increasingly wealthy, discriminating, empowered – and often confused and contradictory – individuals.

- The acceleration of the pace of demand. Users, many of whom are becoming accustomed to the rapid response times of e-commerce, want their demands to be satisfied straight away. They are impatient with what seem to them to be the leisurely timetables of delivery of conventional design, construction and real estate.

- Many consumers, both in housing and design, are genuinely uncertain about what kind of environments they want today. They are even less sure how their lifestyles and work styles will develop in the future.

- Consumers are more mobile. They don't stay in the same street or the same office. Within and between the workplace they are always on the move. They are always moving on.

- More sophisticated ways of managing the housing stock and office space have led, as discussed above, to the professionalisation of the procurement process and of facilities management. These developments have many operational advantages but have not necessarily simplified the relationship between the consumers and the suppliers of the built environment.

- Increasingly powerful and reliable information technology is being exploited to cope with accelerating changes in user demand in both housing and offices. Buildings have begun to be equipped with electronic devices that, in effect, are designed to anticipate user needs. Examples include security systems, lift control devices, environmental controls. The potential for integrated building intelligence, capable of responding to increasingly sophisticated user demands, is immense.

All of these factors are tending to change the balance of power between the providers and the consumers of housing and office space.

Comparative trends in the design of offices and housing

Of the two building types, offices and housing, the design of the office has changed more under user pressure over the last decade. This is probably because of:

- more integrated and responsive decision making in office organisations

- more rapid take-up of information technology in the working environment

- quicker access, in the context of globalising commerce, to innovative international precedents

- more competitive pressure

- greater and more concentrated financial resources being available in the office sector.

For architects and interior designers, an important long-term trend in office design has been a shift from reliance on problem solving (acoustics, cable management, environmental services, work-style choices) by the longer-term, architectural elements – the building shell and building services – to the shorter-life interior-design elements of scenery and settings. Over the life of an office building, far more money is spent on interior design than on architecture. Hence, it is arguable that in office design architecture has become, economically if not operationally or in terms of professional prestige, a branch of interior design.

The same trend exists in a more disguised form in housing design. Users, of course, generally continue to take responsibility for furnishing their own homes out of their own personal budgets. Consequently, it is harder to quantify the underlying shift. However, it is clear that standards of interior design have risen sharply, at least in the private housing sector. I suspect that economic pressures have reduced relative expenditure on housing construction as opposed to housing fit out. Lifestyle choices certainly dominate a large proportion of the weekend newspapers. Consumers seem to want to shape their own environments more and more and the fragmented nature of the housing stock encourages them to do so. It is fascinating to speculate on the possible impact on office design of the increasing empowerment of office workers who may well come to demand a similar degree of choice in work style as they enjoy in their domestic lifestyles.

Another important shift at the more established end of the office market continues to be towards very large, highly serviced and highly specialised office buildings – such as those found in Canary Wharf, in the City of London and in the Thames Valley. However, the spread of information technology could be warning us that this may be the end of a trend. There is already a countervailing tendency for smaller, often more rapidly growing, enterprises to occupy more marginal properties, often in redundant buildings or in new industrial premises, not specifically designed as offices, that offer the big volumes that help to meet shorter and shorter term operational demands. Such buildings are sometimes more permeable than conventional offices, following an important trend towards much more networked and interdependent ways of doing business. It should be said, however, that, with very few exceptions, office developers in the UK and North America have not interested themselves very much in increasing the diversity of the office stock. My impression is that most innovative office design has been created without much help from conventional property development.

Equivalent trends in housing design are towards:

- a wider range of types of housing and housing locations

- the emergence of loft buildings and of conversions – i.e. the appropriation of whatever comes to hand in the inner city, including obsolescent office buildings, to satisfy emerging lifestyle expectations

- the dissolution of conventional locational patterns, so that, in the inner cities at least, quite violent juxtapositions of living, working, retailing, entertainment are now occurring.

The third, and perhaps the most important, shift in office design is the direct consequence of the new ubiquity of information technology. Networks of one kind or another – broadband at an international level, wireless within and between offices – mean that certain long-standing assumptions about where, how and when work is done are increasingly under question. Office workers can now carry the entire database of their whole office around in their laptops and have unlimited access to the whole world at any time from their mobile phones. The design consequences of these new technological capabilities are:

- much more user choice of work settings, within the office and outside

- more mobility within the office, leading to a greater proportion of space given over to collective activities rather than individual workstations

- more strategically located spaces ('streets', 'forums', 'market-places') within the office, all designed to encourage interdisciplinary and interdepartmental interaction.

It is quite possible that the whole direction of office work will change within this decade. The office is likely to become a much more social place. One metaphor that is often used is that the office in an increasingly virtual world will become more like a club, an attractive place, with many amenities, designed, in a much less formally programmed way, to support much higher levels of social and intellectual interaction.

A domestic consequence of these changes is the invasion of the home by the office – and, to a somewhat lesser extent, the invasion of the office by domestic standards. Office work no longer depends upon co-location or even upon synchrony. Consumers will be free to choose to work when and where they want. Hence, the home environment and the domestic timetable will have to be redesigned (and perhaps already should have been designed) to accommodate a substantial component of individual office work that may no longer be carried out 'at work'. In design terms, this means:

- higher environmental standards to support more individual concentrated work

- more space at home to accommodate the workplace activities of one or more partners or family members

- the intrusion of office standards of ergonomics and furniture design, as well as other heath and safety matters, into the home;

- better IT infrastructures in the domestic environment.

At the urban scale, of course, the implications of the dissolution of the nine to five working day and the five-day working week are huge, changing the criteria for the design of transportation systems (e.g. through evening out commuting peaks) and encouraging different, and perhaps more integrated, patterns of location of housing and offices.

Comparative trends in the procurement and management of offices and housing

While an improvement over the last two decades in the standards of professionalism of procuring and managing office space has already been noted, these improvements have often been skewed towards making the supplier's life easier rather than the consumer's. The provision of office space has long been a corporate responsibility and is, in consequence, much less sensitive to the inevitably increasing demands and higher expectations of increasingly mobile, independent and empowered end users than it ought to be.

I suspect that the provision of housing in the UK, both in the public and the private sectors, is similarly biased in favour of the convenience – and profit – of the supplier. The exception is that consumers of housing unlike consumers of office space – up to today – have always enjoyed more control over their own, highly localised, interior environments. Hence, the continuing importance in the domestic market of home furnishings, of home stores and home decorating, and of the whole vast apparatus of DIY. The potential influence of the domestic consumer choice on the office market is indicated by the Swedish furniture manufacturer IKEA's recent success in developing simple, elegantly designed, office furniture which can be bought in knock-down form, not just for the home market, but also for smaller, and indeed as it has turned out, some not so small office organisations. Here, the logistics of mass retailing are beginning to challenge the hegonomy of specialised office furniture manufacturers.

Three other innovations in the management of office space are interesting in that they use a non-office model to address rising user expectations. The first is 'hoteling', i.e. the provision of office space within large organisations on the basis that office users, increasingly mobile as they are, can be treated as if they were guests in a hotel rather than wage slaves tied to their desks.

The metaphor comparing the office with the hotel has profound implications for the procurement and management of office space. Instead of the old economy way of allocating office space by grade or status, the idea that has been taken up with such enthusiasm by businesses such Accenture (formerly Andersen Consulting) is that increasingly mobile office workers will willingly share the expensive resource of office space. This is provided that the users are guaranteed much higher levels of service (e.g. properly trained receptionists and a concierge to deal with personal chores) as well as access to a much wider and richer range of work settings. In this way, a minor real estate miracle is performed. Better service is provided to more people in less space for less money – less money per person accommodated that is, not necessarily less money per square feet.

The second innovation is the serviced offices provided by Regus, and by other similar providers, not just to representative offices of foreign companies but also increasingly to larger organisations that are growing and changing so rapidly that they need instant access to large amounts of fully equipped and manned office accommodation. The novelty of this concept from a real estate point of view is that the customers are willing to pay a lot more for services by the minute rather than for square feet by the year – a much more 'new economy' approach.

The third level of innovation is the wholesale handing over of a government department's stock of space to consortia of private sector providers through private finance initiatives (PFIs) or the similar, and equally attractive, outsourcing of non-core assets, such as office accommodation, that is taking place in the private sector.

For housing, the implications of these new approaches are as follows:

- Rising consumer expectations will affect not just the type of accommodation that is provided but also the means by which it is provided and managed through time.

- Diversity of demand is not just a matter of a widening variety of housing type, size or quality but also implies providing access to a wider range of services.

- Consumer expectations of quicker responses to their housing needs will force housing providers to rethink leasing structures and modes of payment, shifting property from being an asset to becoming a service.

Methodological consequences

In the 1960s, where this essay started out, monolithic supply-side attitudes dominated the design, delivery and management of both housing and offices. Changing lifestyles and aspirations at home and work have made such attitudes unsustainable. The biggest consequence for and the greatest commonality between housing and offices have been on the ways in which architects and designers are being drawn into dependence on new methodologies for involving large numbers of consumers and users in the design process. Such popular involvement has been done in ways that are compatible with achieving longer-term visions for improving the quality not just of the built environment but also of everyone's life in the UK.

Techniques used in both housing and office design include:

- surveys of trends

- workshops and focus groups to involve users in the design process

- scenario planning to test alternative designs

- mock-ups and simulations to make what is being proposed accessible

- change management to ensure not just that the value of design is widely understood but also that the process of design and delivery is used by visionary local authorities (in the case of housing) and by visionary business enterprises (in the case of offices) as the means by which cultural and social change is effected.

There is a big and critically important difference in the way in which user-orientated performance measurement techniques have been applied in offices and housing. In office design, there is a rough equivalence between performance measures of building supply – e.g. the building appraisal techniques that are used to measure the capacity of office buildings to accommodate change – and measures of demand – e.g. techniques such as workplace performance studies (WPS) that are used to assess end-user requirements. In housing there is no such balance. Private sector market research, such as it is, has concentrated on measuring demand. The Housing Quality Indicators recently developed by DEGW are a rare example of measures of the capacity of individual homes, of housing estates, or of the housing stock as a whole to accommodate changing user needs. This simple but fundamental methodological difference may have profoundly limited the ability of housing designers and housing managers to respond to change.

An image of a mixed-use city

An image of a highly desirable but hitherto unattainable kind of urban environment will serve to end this chapter. The image is of the physical consequences of the convergence between two building types that is my underlying message.

Imagine an apartment in a mews at the top end of Marylebone Lane in the West End of London on a sunny summer evening. The half door on the first floor of a former stable is wide open and, looking down the mews at the complex of property that surrounds it, what do I see?

- an agglomeration of property, built up on a medieval street pattern, some from the eighteenth century, rather more from the nineteenth, some from the early years of the twentieth century

- a vibrant mix of building types crowded together at high density – shops, pubs, apartments, houses, workshops, offices, stables, garages

- an intensely rich and desirable environment that has been capable of absorbing and accommodating change for over 200 years – workshops turned into offices, stables into apartments, pubs into shops, houses into offices, offices into houses

- an environment that is immensely capable of being adapted to accommodate even more change

- an environment that would be totally impossible to replicate today given the planning laws and division of functions that have accreted in the twentieth century.

Huge changes are taking place in our culture, our society and our technology. Housing and offices have been very different but in some respects they are converging. Users in both sectors are demanding more and more from the built environment. Many of the conventions that have shaped twentieth-century cities have separated and divided activities that contemporary consumers would prefer to be connected. Such divisive conventions are unlikely to persist very long into the twenty-first century. Popular opinion makes it clear that they are standing in the way of change.

Conclusions

Consumer pressures and user empowerment are making it essential in both housing and offices, in terms of physical design and of the design, delivery and building management process, to listen to aspirations for new work styles and lifestyles. This means that we must use our imagination to rethink the processes by which we design and manage our buildings.

This chapter began by asking the following three questions:

- Are consumerist pressures stronger in housing or offices?

- Will consumer pressures make housing more like offices or offices more like housing?

- Or will both building types continue to be as separate and distinct as they are today?

Three main conclusions have become clear to me in writing this chapter. The first is that, although in recent years consumerist pressures have been more visible and effective in shaping office buildings and office interiors than housing, recent trends in office design seem likely in the longer term to make office buildings much less distinctive as a building type. Some office buildings may become more like housing. Some may even merge with housing. The second conclusion is that consumerist trends give us reason to expect that much existing practice in design process, delivery and tenure in both housing and offices is unsatisfactory and is likely to become increasingly unpopular. Hence, the third conclusion: the possibility exists today, as never before, for far more creative synergy between the design and delivery of housing and offices.

3 'MIND THE GAP': CUSTOMERS' PERCEPTIONS AND THE GAPS BETWEEN WHAT PEOPLE EXPECT AND WHAT THEY ARE OFFERED

Ritsuko Ozaki

Summary

This chapter introduces the concept of the 'gap analysis', and shows the importance of focusing on the gap between customers' perceptions of what they expect and what they are offered. This is because such a gap determines customers' perceptions of the quality of services and products, and therefore their satisfaction levels. The main focus of the discussion here is the discrepancy in house design, as well as that in the quality of workmanship and service provision, in the private house-building sector. In the conclusions, questions arising from our analysis and lessons for UK house builders are presented.

Introduction

In recent years, customer satisfaction has become a key driver for the private new house-building industry in the UK, and there has been a shift from producer convenience to customer focus (Barlow and Ozaki, 2000). But, are customers satisfied with their house builders' 'customer-focused' practices?

The judgement whether one is satisfied or not is 'relative', not 'absolute'. A judgement is always made about what one *has* relative to some standard (Brown, 2000), in this case, to what one *expected to get*. Therefore, a gap between what customers expect and what has been delivered can be used as a measure of customers' satisfaction levels and, accordingly, of the company's performance. In this respect, it is very important that house builders acknowledge this gap and pay attention to what customers expect; this will enable house builders to perform better and consequently boost their business.

There is a huge literature on customer satisfaction in service provision and the quality of workmanship, and our main focus here is on the design of housing. House design that does not 'fit' the resident's values and lifestyle causes considerable dissatisfaction to the resident. The chapter introduces findings of a survey on customers' house design preferences;[1] these highlight an urgent need for house builders to catch up with customer requirements, which are far more diverse than what is currently on offer.

Naturally, some house builders are positively exploring more customer-oriented ways of doing business and are trying to differentiate themselves from those who have not adopted such practices. However, in this chapter, we look at the broad issue, investigating the general differences between people's perceptions of what they expect and what they are offered.

Before exploring customers' preferences and requirements in house design, we will initially look at this notion of a gap between customers' and house builders' views, and at the significance of analysing it. Next, we briefly discuss the differences between customers' and house builders' perceptions of the quality of housing and service provision. Finally, we will discuss this discrepancy between what customers expect in terms of house design and what house builders offer.

46

Why focus on the 'gap'?

The discrepancies between (a) customers' expectations and experiences, and (b) customers' and providers' perceptions are significantly related to customer satisfaction (Brown and Swartz, 1989). In other words, a gap between 'what customers expect' and 'what a company thinks they expect' determines the customers' perceptions of the quality of services and products. Also, the degree to which the product and service performances meet the purchasers' expectation indicates their satisfaction levels (e.g. Oliver, 1981; Parasuraman *et al.*, 1985, 1988; Patterson and Johnson, 1993). Customers' expectations are determined both by what they want (or need)[2] and by how they want to be treated. They have in mind a certain norm or standard by which they evaluate what they receive (Grönroos, 1990).

This expectation-based measure does appear to match intuitive sense; and the model provides a framework linking service quality, customer satisfaction and their behavioural intention; i.e. high service quality correlates with customers' willingness to use a company's service again, to refer the company to others and to pay a price premium (Parasuraman *et al.,* 1994).

So, as mentioned above, since a customer makes judgements about services and products based on his/her expectations, analysing the gap between customers' aspirations and what has been delivered provides clues as to how house builders have performed and what they should do in order to improve their performance.

In their study, Parasuraman and colleagues (1985) found that in the service industry there were gaps between what company executives *thought* customers expected in a quality service and what customers *actually expected* (see Figure 2.1). For instance, security is a pivotal quality attribute for credit card users, but the executives did not see it as critical. Such a misunderstanding on

Figure 2.1 Expectation–offer gap

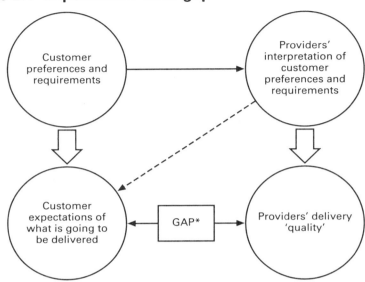

*Expectation–Delivery Quality = GAP

the providers' side is likely to affect (perceived) service quality, and correlates with a propensity to spread negative word-of-mouth communication and with intentions to switch to competitors (Parasuraman *et al.*, 1994).

Winch and colleagues' (1998) research showed that the analysis of this gap in the construction industry led to the delivery of improved value to customers. Through identifying the gaps between customer expectations and the management's perception of customer expectations, and also between the management's perceptions and the *translation* of those perceptions into *specifications*, the firm could reduce guesswork and make a more precise analysis of the construction process. Winch and colleagues concluded that an information flow was the key to success, as it reduced the gap between the customer's and the house builder's views.

These show the importance of understanding the nature of the gap between the perceptions of housing customers and of house builders; a consideration of this gap should be a step forward for house builders.

Research conducted so far in the context of house building has indicated gaps between what customers expect and what house builders offer in three main areas: the quality of workmanship, service provision and house design.

Quality of workmanship

The quality of workmanship is an important satisfaction driver for new home buyers. Some UK house builders have aimed to achieve 'zero defects' in a new house over the first two years of occupancy (Barlow and Gann, 1999). House builders actually provide their customers with a lot of details and advice on their houses, and facilities and appliances that they have installed in them. Information on materials utilised and how to use or look after the facilities, for example, is included in the package that they give to their purchasers. They devote much attention to the quality of the finished products.

Gap

Despite house builders' efforts, however, customers do not seem to be very satisfied with the quality of workmanship of their house; and builders are now required to improve the quality and functionality of the house even more. The Housing Forum's (2000) National Customer Satisfaction Survey found that over 80 per cent of the respondents had reported defects with their new home; about a half of these people claimed that there were *more* defects than they would have expected. Another national survey found that customers thought house builders should take more time and trouble so that the house was *handed over* without faults (Mulholland Research Associates *et al.*, 1999). Similarly, in our survey, the customers of a UK speculative volume house builder complain about the quality of finishes. This contradicts the house builder's views. The staff are confident about the quality of their houses; but the purchasers typically say that their house builder should have better inspection systems before hand-over because there are so many obvious defects, such as missing window locks, poor quality of paintwork, unfinished socket covers and rubbish in the sink. Clearly, their customers would like better quality workmanship than the house builders currently offer. The house builder is now developing an approach using standardised component systems. This will facilitate better quality workmanship in the finished products, as well as a greater level of customer choice, in a cost-effective and sustainable manner.

Service provision

Literature on customer satisfaction emphasises the importance of good quality service provision. This is because good service will make the customer satisfied, and satisfied customers will improve the business through their word-of-mouth referrals and brand loyalty (e.g. Jones and Sasser, 1995; Reichheld and Sasser, 1990). Good quality service includes both pre-purchase and after-sales customer care. Pre-purchase service is closely linked to employees' performance, such as their attentive manner, ability to understand customers' needs and willingness to give information (Hartline and Jones, 1996; Rees Lewis, 1994). After-sales customer care, especially problem resolution, is seen as crucial by customers; and good customer care can be a market differentiator (Mitchell, 1993). Customers who receive effective resolutions to problems become satisfied and have significantly higher loyalty to the company (Zeithaml *et al.*, 1996).

Japanese house builders, for example, are well aware of the importance of service provision, and spend a lot of time with their customers during both pre- and post-purchase periods. They typically hold a few pre-purchase consultation sessions, which even include financial and tax advice. They also pay a few visits after the sale, as well as offering several years' guarantee. In practical terms, after-sales visits provide the house builder with informal feedback, and sometimes word-of-mouth referrals, as well as providing an opportunity to rectify defects. It is important to note that back-up care service which resolves problems quickly helps to make the customer satisfied despite initial defects in the product.

Gap

Some UK house builders have also tried to make efforts to provide better customer care. This includes investment in systems for monitoring complaints, improvement in response times (e.g. using call centres), the appointment of customer care specialists from outside the housing industries, and offering a package of financial and maintenance services.

Nonetheless, a National House Building Council (NHBC) (1997) survey found that 99 per cent of new home purchasers cited poor after-sales service as a major reason for their unwillingness to recommend their house builder. Another national survey (Mulholland Research Associates *et al.*, 1999) revealed that customers felt strongly that house builders should act on their promises and deal with problems immediately. In other words, customers are not satisfied with the services that they receive, feeling that their house builders should look after customers by providing better services.

Similarly, in our survey, the purchasers felt considerable dissatisfaction with the after-care service provided by their house builder. They complained that the house builder did not provide the after-care service as stated on the brochure and that they had to wait for months to get problems and defects sorted out. This house builder, like its competitors, has a customer care centre in each region; however, our survey reveals that their customer care centre does not respond to customers' problems quickly enough. (This house builder is currently establishing a centralised information system, which will be able to deal with such customer information more effectively.) The above illustrates a gap between house builders' professed practices and customers' perceptions of them, and emphasises the importance of service provision.

Design of the house

Just as there are discrepancies between customers' and house builders' views regarding the quality of workmanship and service provision, there are also discrepancies between what people expect and what they have been offered in the area of house design. This is because some designers and architects use only their previous experiences and make assumptions about customers' requirements to draw designs and specifications, rather than including such requirements each time (Dulami *et al.*, 1996), or because information collected from customers is not conveyed properly across sectional boundaries within the organisation (Mohamed and Tucker, 1996).

Nevertheless, there is some movement towards improving house design. Housing Quality Indicators (HQIs) have been developed and tested. These assist in evaluation of location, design and performance on the basis of quality. By using these tools, designers should be able to improve their designs. Similarly, new concepts like 'design for all' or 'barrier-free design' (i.e. design to be as accessible as possible to people with diverse physical abilities) are starting to be adopted in the house-building industry.

'Barrier-free' has become embodied within the UK building regulations. The application of such design practices may help house builders to translate what customers expect into the design of actual houses.

Customers' perceptions of the house

In the UK, the value of a house is partly determined by its size, often defined by the number of rooms. A house is both a property and an investment; its future saleability is important (Ball, 1999) and UK home buyers have specific ideas about what they want to buy. The author's cross-cultural survey on new home-owners (within the English context) revealed that there was a statistically significant difference between English and Japanese home-owners' attitudes (Ozaki, 1999; 2002, forthcoming). English home-owners see the house more materialistically than their Japanese counterparts, with specific ideas about floor plans, the number of bedrooms and the location. English home buyers also see their house as an opportunity for home-based activities, such as gardening and home improvement. The Japanese see the house in more atmospheric terms (e.g. being homely and relaxing, and as an anchor for the family), which reflect their different family values.

House builders' attitudes

So, the question is: how can UK house builders respond to each customer's specific requirements? Research has shown that recession in the housing market in the 1990s led to standardisation of house plans and also to some degree of adaptation of customers' personal preferences in internal layouts, finishes and fittings. However, the accommodation of personal preferences is, to some extent, limited by regulatory, financial and cultural frameworks (Barlow, 1999; Nicol and Hooper, 1999).

House builders do not usually consider that choice of layouts, internal fittings and finishes are a high priority for new house buyers, and do not offer many choices. They complain that the UK home buyers are conservative, because many people worry about the saleability of their house and do not want customised choices, which may detract from the perceived value of their investment. They also claim that this conservatism makes it difficult for them to be innovative in house design (Ball, 1999). Consequently, there have been only a few attempts from the house builders 'to change such conservatism in the ways in which other industries have done through encouraging consumer preferences for their newest products' (Ball, 1999, p. 12).

However, it is important to address each customer's requirements, rather than adopting an 'any colour as long as its black' or 'one size fits all' policy. This is something that many UK and western organisations have taken longer to realise than Japanese and other eastern companies (Stacey, 1992).

Japanese house builders offer a wider range of house design, together with a variety of choices within each design.[3] They manage customers' expectations in a sophisticated way and allow their customers to make decisions about the exterior, floor plan, interior design, and fixtures and fittings. House builders typically provide finished designs on videotape or CD-ROM, so that the customer can get a real image of the home. This is because house builders understand that each customer has a different lifestyle and that a feature that is right for one customer is not right for another. They believe that their job is to offer not only a dwelling, but also a design that suits the customer's life. This involvement of customers in decision making on house design has a great impact on customer satisfaction. People feel more satisfied because they have made their own choice; one is less likely to criticise a design that he/she has contributed to (Mullins, 1999; Tiuri, 2000).

Clearly, UK house builders do not offer as much flexibility in house design as their Japanese counterparts, although the UK house buyers have more specific ideas about their homes.

Customer preferences

Despite UK house builders' belief that their customers do not want customised features, a survey of 1,000 people, carried out by *2000 Homes* in 1999, suggested that 81 per cent of home buyers would like to be offered greater choice over the initial design of their homes. Almost 80 per cent wanted their homes to be more adaptable to accommodate changes in layout at some future stage (Barlow and Gann, 1999). The Housing Forum has also carried out its customer satisfaction survey. Customer satisfaction with house design is one of the issues to be covered. The initial results were published in October 2000 and the 2001 survey results are to be made public in February 2002.

In other words, house builders think customers are conservative and do not want choice. Customers want more choice than house builders offer (which is, perhaps, why they have been unenthusiastic about the choices offered to date) as long as it does not reduce the value of their property.

What kind of choice and flexibility do UK customers want, then? Our survey on housing choice and future needs highlights the diversity of customers' preferences; and this shows that customers are not necessarily conservative and that they want more choice than house builders currently offer.

Two-hundred-and-eight questionnaires were collected from private home-owners. By asking questions with reference to respondents' current and future lifestyle and needs, we have identified housing customers' priorities and preferences.

1 Ground-floor layouts

In the UK, the kitchen has traditionally been the woman's domain and has normally been kept separated from other living spaces (e.g. Darke, 1984; Williams, 1987). However, as women's status improves and formality within the household declines, an open style of kitchen has become more popular (Ozaki, 1999). Some of our respondents prefer an open plan (a kitchen-diner, or sometimes even an all-in-one arrangement). Those with young children and who are elderly find it easier to live in an open-plan house. There are also people who prefer the rooms to be separate, because they sometimes want to shut rooms off. The kitchen is for cooking and the dining room is for eating and entertaining; and some feel that they need space for the adults to sit down and listen to music while the children are watching TV. The preference depends to a large extent on residents' lifecycle stages and associated values. One elderly respondent complained that she and her husband had wanted an open plan, however they could not find a suitable house with such a plan within their range. It would appear that house builders need to offer a greater variety of floor plans.

The position of rooms, as well as their configuration, is an area that divides people's preferences. The front of the house has traditionally been considered to be a public space. People decorate such public parts of the house and hold formal occasions like receiving guests in them. The front room has typically been a place for the display of wealth (e.g. Goffman, 1959; Lunt and Livingstone, 1992). However, not all respondents want their lounge where it would traditionally be, because they feel exposed if the lounge is situated at the front of the house. Some said that they had to draw the curtains early so that people could not look in, although, of course, there are those who said that the lounge should be in the front because it was 'supposed to be there'.

Clearly, there are differences in preferences in room arrangements.

2 Room sizes and layouts

'Spatial trade-offs' – i.e. which room people would like to be largest and how they could compensate by reducing space in other parts of the house – is another area where customers have diverse ideas. For example, a three-bedroom house typically has a master bedroom, a double-bed-sized second bedroom, and a single-bed-sized third bedroom. But, is this size distribution what people want?

There was a comment from a female respondent with two children that she would like to make the third bedroom bigger by reducing the size of other rooms, so that both of her children could have rooms of the same size. Another respondent felt that the second bedroom did not have to be double-bed-sized and she wished she could take some space from there and make the master bedroom bigger.

Similarly, in terms of the ground floor, one respondent said that his lounge was too small and he would like to make it more spacious at the expense of the hallway space. In short, people's ideas about room sizes and configuration are much more diverse than what is usually offered.

3 Internal finishes

Respondents would also like to have internal finishes to their own tastes, or of better quality. The choices that are currently offered by house builders do not seem to be enough. People like to choose colours and materials to suit their own preferences. In particular, walls and floors are areas about which people want to make their own choice of finish. Some would also like to be able to arrange the position of kitchen units according to their taste.

4   Privacy and security

Privacy and security are big issues. An en-suite bathroom is a must; and most respondents considered the option of having an alarm to be very important. Some have had one installed on their own because it was not available at the purchase point. One female respondent said that she had been disappointed that she was not given this option; she expected to have an alarm, as she had seen one in the show home. Similarly, for some, an entrance hall (a hallway) is one of the criteria for choosing the house and is one of the main things that they like about the house. People feel more private or secure if there is a hall at the front entrance.

5   More storage

There is never enough space for storage in the home and customers feel dissatisfied with what is provided. The majority of our respondents felt that they needed more storage space. On the ground floor, they needed more cupboards in the kitchen and storage space for general household goods such as a vacuum cleaner and an ironing board. Some respondents said that they kept those household goods in the garage because of lack of storage space. The garage is, in general, used as a storage room for household goods (e.g. ironing boards, vacuum cleaners, freezers, gardening tools, sports goods, etc.). Some respondents have never used the garage as a parking space. They feel that it is a good idea to have more storage in the hallway area for coats, shopping bags and so on, as the understairs cupboard and the utility room are too small, if they are there at all.

On the first floor, some would like to have built-in cupboards not only in the master bedrooms but also in the smaller rooms. Most respondents would appreciate fitted cupboards and built-in wardrobes, and feel that the option to have more storage space is essential. However, there are some respondents who would prefer their own furniture, because the finishes and design of fitted cupboards and wardrobes are not 'right'. Thus, what should be offered are optional storage spaces and a choice of fitted cupboard designs.

6   Garden size and finishes

People have diverse ideas about their garden and are not particularly satisfied with what has been offered by house builders. An increase in size means an increase in price, so people have to prioritise. Most respondents like to have basic finishes as a starting point from which they can do whatever they like. Some like a large or private garden without any landscaping; and others like a small, but landscaped and maintenance-free garden. To offer quality in a garden means to offer variety and make an attempt to accommodate individual customers' expectations.

Similarly, some think that the customer should be consulted over the choice of finish in the front garden (e.g. being paved, a lawn, having more trees) and the position of the driveway. Some feel that they need more privacy and would like more mature shrubs for privacy or small fences to mark the boundary because their neighbours cut across, or park cars on, their land.

7   Lifestyle and life-cycle-stages: future needs and flexibility

Lastly, people's lifestyles change according to their life-cycle stages. Starting a family, working from home and ageing are the most common lifestyle changes. In this regard, people would like more flexibility in the use of space. For those who anticipate an expansion in household composition, such extra space as a conservatory would provide an ideal extra living area; and 'habitable' roof space would be a good extra room for a study, a child's room, or a guest room.

Those who work from home, or are thinking of it, are attracted to integrated facilities that allow them to use a computer and internet services in their home. More typically, extra electrical sockets and telephone and television points are required in accordance with an increase in the use of consumer durables like video recorders and computers. Some of our respondents have paid extra to put in more sockets, telephone points and lighting (e.g. in the kitchen, garage, loft, or outside), or to put sockets or switches in the right places for them. They would like their house builder to provide either as many sockets and points as possible or an option to locate these service points wherever they like in their house.

For older generations, ageing is a serious issue. They feel that they will need low or easy maintenance and a downstairs bedroom (or to live at one level). One elderly couple said that they had not bought a bungalow, as there had been only a limited range of design in bungalows, and had not been able to find the right house for them. This means that a wider range of house plans in one house type is required, as well as a better mix of housing types.

Gap

These findings clearly show the diversity of customers' requirements and that they want more variety than is offered. One of the reasons for most people choosing to buy second-hand housing is that they gain more choice over design, as well as choice over location and higher space standards (Barlow and Gann, 1999). What house builders currently deliver does not cover all the requirements, and customers would appreciate a wider range, or more flexibility, in house design. Such gaps can cause dissatisfaction on the customer's part. As one of our respondents said, if customers cannot find the 'right' house design for them within the design range of a house builder, they simply do not buy a house from that company; there are other house builders in the area.

Conclusions

This chapter has highlighted the fact that there are gaps between what customers expect and what is currently offered. These gaps are present not only in service provision and the quality of workmanship, but also in the design of housing. People would like more choice than is currently offered; they would, at least, like to have an opportunity to think about alternatives that would be more suitable to their lives.

This is a very important issue for every house builder. As Winch and colleagues' (1998) study showed, acknowledging and analysing the gap between what they offer and what customers expect enables house builders to deliver value to each customer and, thereby, improve their business.

Seen this way, it is essential to identify customers' priorities and understand their requirements in the prioritised areas in order to bridge the gap between house builders' and customers' views about house design. House builders should conduct comprehensive market research, including questionnaire surveys, interviews and informal feedback from both customers and front-line workers who have everyday contact with the customers (Heskett *et al.*, 1997). Discussions between the house builder and the customer are particularly important. This reduces misunderstanding on the house builder's part about the customer's design preferences and requirements, and consequently the discrepancy between the two sides' views. Efforts have to be made to close these gaps; this is the best, if not the only, way to make customers happy, and therefore improve business.

Through our analyses of the gap between what people expect and what they are offered in house design, a number of issues regarding the size and layout of houses have arisen.

- Although the number of bedrooms is a determinant of house value, there has been a change in that some house builders have started to use a numeric indicator of floor space. This is a more accurate measure and responds in part to people's demand to have more space in the house. Space is a major issue for housing customers.

- The issues of room size (space) and layout are entangled. The need for a trade-off between size and layout is always a problem.

- Horizontal and vertical layout also needs to be considered. Ageing, for example, often requires an increased horizontal use of space, whereas the expansion of family means householders may need extra space, for example, in the roof.

- The use of design tools and guides, such as Housing Quality Indicators (HQIs), may facilitate an improvement in quality. Not only are size and layout measured, but also other issues can be considered such as light and services, accessibility, energy and sustainability issues, and performance in use.

These issues offer us a framework within which we can move forward in terms of customer-focused performance.

There are, of course, a great many unresolved questions that require future research, including the following issues.

- There is more to explore in terms of demands, as each segment in the housing market, together with various regions and cultures, has different requirements. More detailed understanding of what customers expect could lead to the provision of flexibility in housing with increasing choice for customers (see Gann *et al.,* 1999). A value-choice model and option packages to cover the issue of trade-offs need to be developed.

- Regulatory frameworks may set limits to offering choice, but how much and in what aspects still needs to be investigated.

- The establishment of customer centres, as in Japan, may help house builders to capture and understand what people expect.

- The integration of the design process with sales and marketing (including receiving feedback) could help to close the 'loop'. This is also a learning process for house builders whereby they can develop and improve their designs.

To conclude, this gap analysis approach offers several lessons for UK house builders.

- Market research helps house builders to identify what customers really expect in house design as well as service and workmanship. This is an issue that needs to be grasped by the UK house-building industry.

- Customers have their priority list. Finding out what housing attributes they consider to be important enables house builders to offer choice and flexibility in house design.

- People are more committed to a decision that they have had a part in. They are more satisfied not only because they have been given a choice, but also because they have a greater sense of ownership of the finished product.

Acknowledgements

I would like to thank the EPSRC and DETR for funding the MCNS (Meeting Customer Needs through Standardisation) project through which survey data were collected. My thanks also go to our project partners, Cardiff University's Logistics Systems Dynamics Group and nine industrial partners. I am grateful to David Gann and John Rees Lewis for their helpful comments on earlier drafts of this paper, and to the Joseph Rowntree Foundation for giving me this opportunity to write on customer experiences in UK housing. Finally, I wish to thank the questionnaire respondents and interview informants.

Notes

1   This survey was conducted as a part of a major research project funded by DETR, EPSRC and a number of industrial partners.

2   There is a large body of literature on the subjectivity of needs and wants (e.g. Lunt and Livingstone, 1992) which requires deeper understanding in the housing context. This is the subject of future work; in this chapter, we use the term 'expectations'.

3   It should be noted that 75 per cent of newly built houses in Japan are commissioned by individuals and built on their own plot of land. The remaining 25 per cent are built speculatively for sale and the purchasers are given little choice (Barlow and Ozaki, 2001).

References

Ball, M. (1999) 'Chasing a snail: innovation and housebuilding firms' strategies', *Housing Studies*, Vol. 14, No. 1, pp. 9–22

Barlow, J. (1999) 'From craft production to mass customisation. Innovation requirements for the UK housebuilding industry', *Housing Studies*, Vol. 14, No. 1, pp. 23–42

Barlow, J. and Gann, D. (1999) 'Searching for customer focus in UK house building', paper presented at the CIB Conference on Customer Focus in Construction, Cape Town, 5–10 September

Barlow, J. and Ozaki, R. (2000) 'User needs, customisation and new technology in UK house building', paper presented at the ENHR 2000 conference, Gävle, Sweden, 26–30 June

Barlow, J. and Ozaki, R. (2001) 'Are you being served? Japanese lessons on customer focused housebuilding', report of a Department of Trade and Industry Expert Mission, Science and Technology Policy Research Unit (SPRU), the University of Sussex

Brown, R. (2000) *Group Processes*, 2nd edn. Oxford: Blackwell.

Brown, S.W. and Swartz, T.A. (1989) 'A gap analysis of professional service quality', *Journal of Marketing*, Vol. 53, pp. 92–8

Darke, J. (1984) 'House design and women's roles', in Matrix (ed.) *Making Spaces: Women and the Man-made Environment*. London: Pluto Press

Dulami, M., Baxendale, A. and Jewell, M. (1996) 'Refocusing construction to meet customers' requirements', in D. Langford and A. Retik (eds) *The Organization and Management of Construction: Shaping Theory and Practice*. London: E. & F.N. Spon

Gann, D., Biffin, M., Connaughton, J., Dacey, T., Hill, A., Moseley, R. and Young, C. (1999) *Flexibility and Choice in Housing*. Bristol: The Polity Press

Goffman, E. (1959) *The Presentation of Self in Everyday Life*. New York: Doubleday

Grönroos, C. (1990) *Service Management and Marketing: Managing the Moments of Truth in Service Competition*. Lexington, MA: Lexington Books

Hartline, M.D. and Jones, K.C. (1996) 'Employee performance cues in a hotel service environment: influence on perceived service quality, value, and word-of-mouth intentions', *Journal of Business Research*, Vol. 35, pp. 207–15

Heskett, J.L., Sasser, W.E., Jr and Schlesinger, L.A. (1997) *The Service Profit Chain: How Leading Companies Link Profit and Growth to Loyalty, Satisfaction, and Value*. New York, The Free Press

(The) Housing Forum (2000) *First National Customer Satisfaction Survey: Key Findings*. London: The Housing Forum

Jones, T.O. and Sasser W.E., Jr (1995) 'Why satisfied customers defect', *Harvard Business Review*, Vol. 73, November–December, pp. 88–99

Lunt, P.K. and Livingstone, S.M. (1992) *Mass Consumption and Personal Identity*. Milton Keynes: Open University Press

Mitchell, V.W. (1993) 'Handling consumer complaint information: why and how?' *Management Decision*, Vol. 31, No. 3, pp. 21–8

Mohamed, S. and Tucker, S. (1996) 'Options for applying BPR in the Australian construction industry', *International Journal of Project Management*, Vol. 14, No. 6, pp. 379–85

Mulholland Research Associates, House Builders' Federation and Halifax (1999) *Housing Market Research 1999: Consumer Confidence, Home Working, and Customer Care*. London: The Housing Forum

Mullins, L.J. (1999) *Management and Organisational Behaviour*, 5th edn. London: Pitman

National House Building Council (NHBC) (1997) *The New Housing Monitor. Summary Report for the Top 22 Builders*. Amersham: National House Building Council

Nicol, C. and Hooper, A. (1999) 'Contemporary change and the housebuilding industry: concentration and standardisation in production', *Housing Studies*, Vol. 14, No. 1, pp. 57–76

Oliver, R.L. (1981) 'Measurement and evaluation of satisfaction processes in retail settings', *Journal of Retailing*, Vol. 57, pp. 25–48

Ozaki, R. (1999) 'Society, culture and housing form in England and Japan', doctoral thesis, the University of Sussex

Ozaki, R. (2002, forthcoming) 'Housing as a reflection of culture: privatised living and privacy in England and Japan', *Housing Studies*

Parasuraman, A., Zeithaml, V. and Berry, L. (1985) 'A conceptual model of service quality and its implications for future research', *Journal of Marketing*, Vol. 49, pp. 41–50

Parasuraman, A., Zeithaml, V. and Berry, L. (1988) 'SERVQUAL: a multiple-item scale for measuring consumer perceptions of service quality', *Journal of Retailing*, Vol. 64, pp. 12–40

Parasuraman, A., Zeithaml, V.A. and Berry, L.L. (1994) 'Moving forward in service quality research: measuring different customer-expectation levels, comparing alternative scales, and examining the performance–behavioral intentions link', *Marketing Science Institute Working Paper Report*, pp. 94–114, Cambridge, MA

Patterson, P.G. and Johnson, L.W. (1993) 'Disconfirmation of expectations and the gap model of service quality: an integrated paradigm', *Journal of Consumer Satisfaction, Dissatisfaction and Complaining Behavior*, Vol. 6, pp. 90–9

Rees Lewis, J. (1994) 'Patient views on quality care in general practice: literature review', *Social Science in Medicine*, Vol. 39, No. 5, pp. 655–70

Reichheld, F.F. and Sasser, W., Jr (1990) 'Zero defections: quality comes to services', *Harvard Business Review*, Vol. 68, pp. 105–11

Stacey, R.D. (1992) *Managing the Unknowable: Strategic Boundaries between Orders and Chaos in Organizations*. San Francisco: Jossey-Bass

Tiuri, U. (2000) 'Open building concept and recent practice', *Open House International*, Vol. 25, No. 1, pp. 34–43

Williams, P. (1987) 'Constituting class and gender: a social history of the home, 1700–1901', in N. Thrift and P. Williams (eds) *Class and Space: The Making of Urban Society*. London: Routledge & Kegan Paul

Winch, G., Usmani, A. and Edkins, A. (1998) 'Towards total project quality: a gap analysis approach', *Construction Management and Economics*, Vol. 16, pp. 193–207

Zeithaml, V.A., Berry, L.L. and Parasuraman, A. (1996) 'The behavioral consequences of service quality', *Journal of Marketing*, Vol. 60, April, pp. 31–46

4 DESIGNING FOR FUTURE HOMES WITH A REUNDERSTANDING OF THE PAST

Julian Hakes[1]

Summary

It is a peculiar feature of the housing market in the UK that so much of our building stock comprises older properties that are continually renewed and enjoyed well past their projected life span. Twenty-first-century consumers who are fortunate enough to have a choice continue to pay a premium for these properties, whether they be country manors, Georgian town houses or humble vernacular cottages. Such houses, particularly of the latter variety, have constituted an idea of 'home' that remains embedded deep in our national psyche. The developers of the twentieth century, despite prolific building, have barely shifted this paradigm. Why? Do these older houses have qualities that are fundamentally more satisfying to the spirit than their newly built equivalents? If this is the case, have these qualities been lost, perhaps irretrievably, so that they are unattainable in the modern context?

This essay will address those two questions. We will contend that, yes, there are special qualities, beyond mere nostalgia, which explain the enduring attraction of older properties. These are *experiential* qualities. While the stylistic trappings of the 'traditional' dwelling continue to be appropriated by modern house builders, these experiential qualities have been lost – but not irretrievably. We will conclude by arguing that, at this moment in time, designers are uniquely well placed to reacquire an experiential understanding of the dwelling. This understanding should bring about a fundamental re-evaluation of the way in which we build houses today.

Two fundamental concepts

There are two concepts that should be central to any discussion of housing: the concept of the 'house' and the concept of the 'dweller'. Although commonplace, these concepts are so fundamental that we must preface our argument by briefly defining them.

'House'

First, 'house' and 'home' are not synonymous. Builders build houses that are physical containers for lives. People attach meanings and memories to these houses, turning them into homes. A good house is a willing receptacle for these meanings:

> We are all of us fascinated by the house. By our own home, of course. It's the place where we live, day after day, year after year. It gives us shelter and comfort, both physically and emotionally. It is where we retreat when we are ill, and it is the place in which we celebrate the major events of our lives. Even more fundamentally, it serves to define who we are and who we are not ... The continual reconfiguration of our home to cope with our changing needs – we get married, produce children, divorce, remarry and grow older – shapes and celebrates our lives, and provides a physical memory of their course.

> Built on these practical and emotional needs, the house is also the focus of a rich fantasy life of hopes and dreams.
>
> (Sudjic, 1999)

The house is a physical interface between the dweller and the world, connecting/separating the private self with/from nature, climate and the public realm. It is a consumer of resources, expending material and energy in order to provide comfort and convenience. The amount of resources consumed can be seen as a measure of the (in)compatibility of the house with the lifestyle of its occupants. The house is also a part of the built landscape. The spaces between our private houses define the public territory of neighbourhoods and cities.

'Dweller'

The word 'dweller' is carefully chosen, for it suggests a person living in and interacting with a familiar space. In considering the experience of the house, we are concerned primarily with the most basic human attributes that underlie our response to our surroundings. We enjoy the feel of a cool stone surface on a hot day, or the warmth of sunlight through a window on a frosty morning. We respond to light and shade, to our acoustic environment, to enclosure and exposure, to the quality of the air that we breathe.

These unchanging human attributes are overlaid by culturally conditioned lifestyle choices that are diverse and subject to rapid change. Both 'humanness' and 'lifestyle' should guide the design of the house. In the rush to address the latter, we should be careful not to neglect the former.

Learning from old houses

Over the last 25 years, most marketing brochures for speculative housing have contained the word 'traditional'. 'Traditional' has become a style – a hotchpotch of motifs, a pastiche image of an English rural domesticity that is neither sustainable nor appropriate for a culturally diverse modern Britain. This is unfortunate because the authentic tradition of house building in Britain provides many lessons relevant to the present.

The term 'old houses' is a necessary generalisation, referring here simply to properties that are over a century old and continue to be lived in today. We do not wish to idealise such old houses – even less to suggest that any one type can provide a model for the future. However, for the purposes of this discussion, we are content to make reference to an eclectic selection of house types and only to their best qualities, that is, those qualities that might hold lessons relevant to current housing issues.

Through our work, we have identified what we consider to be the essential elements in the experience of a house. These provide the framework for the following exploration.

Space

Major assumptions about lifestyle are implicit within modern industry space standards. We know that the furniture requirements of a master bedroom are: a double bed, a chair, a dressing table and his/her wardrobes. We plan a room that can be used in this way – the trouble is that often it can be used *only* in this way. The same is true for all of the other rooms. Houses therefore become an assemblage of distinct rooms, each to be used in a prescribed manner. Such houses are less able to accommodate changing lifestyles or demographic realities and thus cannot contribute to a sustainable building stock.

One way of dealing with the increasing diversity of family size and lifestyle is an 'open building' approach, as exemplified by many of the new Dutch developments. Here, the occupiers are essentially faced with a large unfinished space to make their own. There are benefits to this approach, but often the spaces provided are very neutral, requiring the dweller to make a great deal of effort to inhabit and personalise them. However, unfinished spaces do not have to be neutral.

One element of the 'character' of old houses is that their spaces are richly suggestive of use without necessarily being prescriptive. The best examples contain a variety of not only sizes of space, but also conditions that are open to individual interpretation. We may, for example, choose to eat, read, or sleep in a specific place because of a particular quality of light, sound or material. Learning from this, it is possible to imagine something between the standard plan and the open plan that is much more flexible than the standard plan. It provides a number of different conditions within linked spaces and therefore enables a variety of activities to co-exist or overlap.

Now that we are being encouraged to build and live more densely on brownfield sites, the interface of private and public spaces requires careful consideration. Perceived concerns about privacy and security often lead developers to install fences and security cameras that erode the public realm and reduce opportunities for social interaction at a neighbourhood level. However, a typical London street of terraced houses offers some obvious lessons. The street is self-policing as it is always overlooked. The living spaces of the houses are often removed from pavement level by half a storey, or separated from the pavement by a light well, thus affording the occupier some privacy and security. The entrance steps provide a transitional space between public and private. The resulting hierarchy of spaces allows the dweller to exercise choice as to their level of engagement with the community.

Comfort and contact with nature

Owners often cite 'contact with nature' as the main attraction of the suburban lifestyle. Our relationship with nature is mediated through the filter of the building envelope. Therefore, if we make compact living on brownfield sites an attractive option, the fundamental human need for contact with nature must guide every stage of the design process.

We have become accustomed to a degree of comfort in our homes that exerts an unacceptably high cost on the planet's resources. Developers are finally being forced to build more energy-efficient houses, and two distinct approaches are emerging. The first is the so-called 'intelligent building' which, at its best, uses technology to enable the building to respond automatically to changes in weather or occupancy in an attempt to ensure maximum efficiency and comfort.

The second approach owes a great deal to vernacular buildings, in which an understanding of the micro-climate of the site informs design decisions, from orientation and placement down to detail and choice of materials. Of course, the vernacular builder had an intuitive understanding of the place, acquired through a lifetime's experience. We do not have that advantage but, as will be explained later, we do now have available the tools that can help us to achieve that same sensitivity.

The result of this approach is inevitably a dwelling of individuality, rooted in its particular context. From site strategy down to intimate detail, it will be designed to ensure the greatest possible energy benefit from the natural environment. The south façade may have large glazed openings and be shaded from the summer sun with louvres and overhangs to avoid overheating.

Insulated shutters for night-time use may be introduced, to retain heat and provide security. The north walls may be heavily insulated with small, carefully placed openings. Solid internal construction, perhaps masonry, may act as a thermal store, absorbing solar energy by day and emitting it by night. This time-lag effect, which is so common in old houses, reduces uncomfortable swings in internal temperature. A constant and comfortable level of humidity may be achieved by choosing natural, porous finishes that absorb and release moisture, such as clay plaster. Ventilation and light may be controlled by the manual opening and closing of windows, shutters and louvres, which also moderate visual and acoustic privacy. Thus, the dweller is constantly engaged in an active relationship with the natural environment. The pleasure of contact with nature is celebrated – even within an urban context.

Materials and construction

We seem to have a special affinity for the natural, 'real' materials of old buildings. We look at a stone wall and we instinctively know that it will feel hard and solid, be acoustically reflective, and feel warm if it has been in the sun and perhaps cool if it has not. We expect timber to smell and feel like wood, and a timber floorboard to creak in a particular way. Thus, in an old house, different material qualities combine with qualities of climate and space to create a sensory experience of great variety – one which we can relate to intuitively.

Few new houses provide a sensory experience of such richness and the use of materials that do not behave according to natural logic is disorienting. A plasterboard wall feels neutral to the touch and, whilst being acoustically reflective, sounds hollow despite its solid appearance. A laminate surface feels neither warm nor cool regardless of whether it looks like stone or like wood. The typical new house is a desensitised environment where the prevailing smell is of unnatural chemicals from paints and glues.

Current research suggests that the internal environment of a new-build home is often ten times more polluted than the external environment. Many materials contain petrochemical derivatives which are slowly released into the environment as the materials begin to deteriorate during their life. This is proven to have a detrimental effect on the health of the occupants – it is, for example, often cited as a cause of the increase in child asthma and allergies. There are alternatives and non-harmful natural materials are readily available. These are often the materials of the traditional dwelling, such as clay render, natural paints and unfired brick. It is a misconception that natural materials are necessarily expensive and requiring of specialist skills. On the continent, these materials have been formed into products that are suited to the needs of the modern construction industry and, as house builders commit to their large-scale use, the prices could become comparable with conventional building technology.

We have already discussed the need for houses to be able to adapt to accommodate fast-changing lifestyles, as well as changes in the family situation. Old houses that are still lived in today survive because they have facilitated such adaptation. A terraced house exhibits an orderly facade to the street while, at the rear, it provides a disorderly expression of the individuality of each of its occupants, past and present. In terms of construction, this is what we referred to earlier as suggestive (rather than prescriptive or neutral) building. The clear territorial division of the solid party walls and the immutability of the facade suggest that backwards, upwards or downwards is the way that the house should expand. The immediately comprehensible structural logic and the basic construction technology mean that transformation is conceivable to most occupants and within the abilities of most local builders. Once the durable architectural framework is established, an almost vernacular process of continuing adaptation can take place, with the work remaining within the local community.

How does this observation relate to the major advances in prefabricated building technology that are currently being pioneered in the UK? We are wary about the wide use of prefabrication because it could result in a transferral of the power of adaptation away from the dweller and the local community into the hands of specialist companies. This may extinguish the small-scale, organic transformation of neighbourhoods by which cities have evolved throughout history. It may also produce buildings of short life spans, because of the eventual redundancy of factory-made components. If we are to exploit the enormous potential of prefabrication, we believe it is necessary to develop a system that, once assembled, behaves as conventional construction, thus facilitating easy adaptation and incremental renewal.

Detail

Much of our enjoyment of old houses comes from the things that we touch. In the erosion of a stone step, we feel that we are treading a path that many feet have trodden before. We enjoy running our hand along a wooden banister that has been worn smooth by generations of use. There is something deeply reassuring about the way in which these 'real' materials weather – a sense of permanence and continuity.

These 'real' materials have their own inherent detail (the grain of wood, the strata of stone), as well as their own discipline of construction detailing (such as timber jointing techniques). It is these details, as well as the ornament of some old properties, that mediates between the scale of the dweller and the scale of the building.

Learning the lessons now

From the above discussion, we conclude that the enduring popularity of old houses resides primarily in the quality of *experience* that they provide. The characteristics that we have described add up to a relationship – an interaction between the dweller and the house. This is a fundamentally different understanding of tradition from that which has given rise to the 'traditional-style' new-build house. These lessons should transcend time and fashion, but they are particularly apt at this moment in time, as house builders are searching for a new direction to suit our millennial desire for innovation.

Volume builders have turned to designers with the question, 'What should the twenty-first-century house be like?' This challenge presents us with an opportunity to demonstrate the 'added value' that good design can bring to the industry but it also poses great dangers, for the question anticipates a *reinvention* of the dwelling.

Only the dweller can 'reinvent' the dwelling, just as only society can change the city. Designers are not social engineers – we respond to and reflect society far more than we influence it. Where singular visions of 'new' ways of living have been imposed upon society, such as the tower blocks of the 1960s, they have either failed, or succeeded only through the creativity of their users who have adapted their spaces and imbued them with meaning in defiance of the whole. A comprehensive 'reinvention' of the dwelling is therefore out of the question. However, for house builders, the *idea* of 'reinvention' is a tempting marketing device, particularly within such a media-driven industry. The 'reinvented' house might be simply a new style – the superficial image of a high-tech 'intelligent' building replacing the superficial image of English vernacular. This is a good moment to relearn the lessons from our house-building heritage.

Reconnecting

> Vernacular buildings are not the sentimental, picturesque backdrop to real life. They may be beautiful but that is beside the point. They have emerged out of hard necessities, hard work and hard lives. Their appeal lies in the sense that they make. The vernacular tradition is dead and cannot be resurrected. It is for home truths, general principles and the indulgence of the eye that we value it. We are the fortunate heirs to this wealth.
>
> (Darley, 1983)

Having highlighted the qualities that make old houses so appealing we can now address the second question that we posed at the start of this essay: have these qualities been lost, perhaps irretrievably, so that they are unachievable in the modern context?

We suggest that the answer is 'no'. While the vernacular builder may indeed be consigned to history, there are some compelling reasons for believing that the qualities that we have been admiring in old buildings are both achievable and viable in the twenty-first century.

The environmental imperative

The first reason is the environmental imperative. Tighter regulations on carbon dioxide emissions and wider public awareness of environmental issues will encourage builders to construct more energy-efficient housing. It will no longer be adequate to produce standard designs that are repeated around the country regardless of context. Houses will have to be designed to take maximum energy benefit from their surroundings, resulting in particular solutions for particular places.

Furthermore, if certification schemes such as BRE (the Building Research Establishment) EcoHomes are to gain wider recognition, builders will have to take a longer-term view of their business in pursuit of a top rating for sustainability. The lifetime building costs including 'embodied energy' will have to be considered – from construction, through use, to demolition and re-use or disposal. This might make it viable to invest more in quality natural materials which would last for longer, would make a healthier internal environment and could be harmlessly disposed of at the end of their life.

New technology

We have admired the way in which a vernacular building works in harmony with its immediate environment to achieve comfort for its occupants. While we do not have the benefit of the vernacular builder's lifelong experience of the locality, we do now have the tools that can enable us to achieve a similar sensitivity to the metabolism of place. In this approach, technology is used as a means to understanding rather than as an end in itself. Analytical and predictive computer models can be used to understand and refine the environmental performance of spaces. The use of techniques such as dynamic thermal simulation, three-dimensional light modelling and computational fluid dynamics enables designers to explore the effect of orientation, opening size and material choice, from the initial concept design through to the refinement of details.

An empowered consumer

The argument for perpetuating the status quo in housing design says that the houses that we build always sell, so why change? The counter-argument says that these houses sell because consumers feel that they have no choice but to buy what is provided, such is the demand.

An empowered consumer is an essential prerequisite of a healthy, competitive housing market. As the internet becomes used increasingly as a vehicle for marketing houses, potential buyers will at last be able to make a fully informed judgement about their investment. The watercolour image of the facade will be superseded by the virtual walk through. Buyers will be able to explore the interior of the house as it will look at any time and in any season. Environmental modelling will enable them to quickly grasp how the house works environmentally and to understand the consequences of their choices in terms of energy use, lifetime cost and comfort. Eventually, we may choose houses as we do other products, balancing build quality, durability and efficiency against short-term cost.

Conclusion

The United Kingdom possesses a rich tradition of house building. We have argued here for a fundamental reunderstanding of that tradition, emphasising that it is the *experiential* qualities of old houses, not simply their appearance, which have guaranteed their popularity and longevity. It is these qualities that give us satisfaction as human beings and allow the house to truly become a home.

The essence of traditional building is that it has always evolved, in a constant negotiation between the dweller, their lifestyle and the material and climatic resources of the place. Therefore, a design approach for today with the concerns that we have identified at its core will produce a building stock that may look quite different from the so-called 'traditional' style, and will make appropriate use of new technologies. It will, however, remain absolutely true to the principles that have underlain house building for centuries, fulfilling our human needs and bringing us closer to nature in a healthy, clean, compact urban future.

Note

1   Tim Bradley and Cari-Jane Hakes as co-authors.

References

Darley, G. (1983) *Built in Britain*. London: Weidenfeld & Nicholson
Sudjic, D. (1999) *Home – the Twentieth-century House*. London: Laurence King

5 IMPROVING THE IMAGE OF NEW HOUSES

Raymond Young

Summary

Around 10 per cent of all house sales are new homes. Consumers appear to prefer older houses, to lack confidence in the new house building industry and to be uncertain about the value for money of new houses. While little research has been carried out into consumer attitudes towards new versus old, anecdotal evidence would lead to the conclusion that there are genuine concerns about a lack of consumer confidence in the market. This lack of confidence applies mainly to the mass-market sector; the growth of other sectors such as conversion, 'infill' and self-procurement may be an indication that consumers do want greater choice.

Choice in the mass-market sector is influenced by a large number of players on the supply side – including the lending institutions, insurance companies, surveyors, planning authorities and the construction industry – all of which tend to be conservative. With limited published research into what consumers are looking for, the Consumer Preference Surveys carried out by Scottish Homes in the mid-1990s reinforce the commonly held belief that location is the key criterion, along with price and number of bedrooms. Despite small sample size, there is also evidence that consumers are concerned about construction quality, but express it on the basis that they want traditional building processes.

Our culture and our collective psyche may also play an important influence in our attitude towards new houses, and lead to a number of questions.

- What is it about location that is important? Could it be that buying a house in a new and unknown area involves taking a risk with neighbours and neighbourhood that few of us are willing to take?

- Has the volatility of the market made us even more cautious about buying in an untested location?

- Does the industry's marketing approach and lack of long-term customer focus reduce rather than inspire consumer confidence?

- Do we have a deep-rooted psyche that says that real homes have to be made of traditional materials and cannot be prefabricated?

- Do consumers have sufficient knowledge and understanding about what constitutes 'good' design and sustainability to be able to influence the industry? Do we have sufficient confidence to challenge what is provided? Do we need to develop educational programmes through which consumers can become 'intelligent clients'?

In conclusion, evidence of growing consumer demand for more choice in the mass market is difficult to amass, but may be indicated by the growth of a wider range of new house providers – albeit at present targeting niche markets. Consumers appear to place location and cost at the top of their priorities and are not well equipped to act as 'intelligent clients'. Their vision needs to be expanded through popular educational programmes.

Introduction

On the face of it, there is plenty of consumer choice in owner-occupied housing in the UK. There is a flourishing second-hand market and a wide variety of developers providing an array of new house types and styles, at a range of costs and locations. The consumer buys the products and sometimes personalises them through additions (e.g. conservatories) or improvements (e.g. new kitchens or bathroom fittings) and internal or external decoration. Personalisation is carried out by professional companies, 'homers' or DIY.

But there are concerns about consumer choice. These relate primarily to the 'new homes industry' rather than to the second-hand market, and can be summed up as:

- consumers prefer older houses to new ones

- consumers lack confidence in the new homes industry

- consumers question whether they are getting value for money.

In addition, there are wider questions about the quality of the products that are available. These are:

- uniformity

- an outdated building process

- poor architectural design – trying to look old rather than modern

- lack of sustainability.

These concerns are difficult to quantify, indeed there is little research into consumer attitudes towards new versus older housing. But anecdotal evidence would lead to the conclusion that these concerns are in whole or part real.

The new homes market

In 1999, just over 1.1 million houses were sold in England and Wales, of which only 11,698 (9.8 per cent) were new houses. But, even this smaller 'new homes market' is not homogeneous. For the purpose of this chapter, the key sectors can be described as follows:

- *The mass-market sector*: producing about 85 per cent of all new housing in the UK. It is dominated by a small number of national players with a limited range of house types built on 'greenfield' sites (although more are being built on reclaimed or 'brownfield' sites). The key to the process is land assembly and land development. Profits are made largely on the increase in value of the land. Consumer choice is limited to internal finishes within a design that is predetermined by the developer. Most of these developments create large suburban estates with a limited range of house sizes and prices and therefore a neighbourhood of one social class.

- *The conversion sector*: often architect/developer led and small scale. Location mainly in inner city/ex-industrial/commercial areas. Appears to cater for a more 'niche' market and now progressively developing 'lofts' – where the fitting out is left to the purchaser.

- *The 'infill' sector:* small developments in established neighbourhoods. Carried out by smaller local or regional-based developers. Some of these will be the same architect/developers that undertake conversion work and will include 'chic' designer-led developments.

- *The self-procurement sector:* including self-build, either individually or groups. In this market, the consumer acquires the site and arranges for the development to be undertaken – normally by arranging directly with component manufacturers like timber-frame manufacturers who also supply to the developers in the mass market. This may be regarded as the 'top end' of consumer choice – the consumer plays an active part in the design (and construction) process, creating a house that suits both his/her purse and requirements. Because of the difficulty of acquiring sites, particularly in areas of high demand, this tends to be at the upper end of the market or in rural areas. There are regional differences within the UK – the average in the UK as a whole is 6 per cent of the market; in Scotland, this is 9 per cent. This reflects the growth of population in rural areas coupled with the absence of national players outside the main population areas.

Just as there are different providers in these different sectors, so it is likely that the consumers will be different, particularly in terms of their demands and understanding of design and lifestyle. The growth of the non-mass market is the first evidence that consumers are looking for more choice. But it is a niche market – both in terms of providers and consumers.

On this basis, the concerns about consumer choice and product quality are more likely to be in the mass-market sector than the others. The rest of this chapter will concentrate on the mass-market sector.

Influences on the mass-market sector

While there may be little published research into consumer attitudes towards new house building, this does not mean that market research is not being carried out. Individual developers undertake market research as part of their marketing. Developers claim that their products respond to consumer demand. But availability can have a serious effect on what is demanded. The consumer has come to believe that what is offered is what is available. And others also influence what is available:

- *The lending institutions and insurance companies* have a highly conservative influence on the design and construction of the product. Try to get a mortgage or to insure what is described as 'non-traditional', or even slightly out of the ordinary. Even timber frame is regarded as 'non-traditional' by some institutions, despite the fact that nearly 50 per cent of new houses in Scotland are constructed in this way.

- *Valuation surveyors* acting on behalf of lenders take a 'risk-averse' view of products. They are extremely cautious when faced with products that involve new components.

- *Planning authorities* often look for traditional materials and designs rather than encouraging innovation. This may be more at a political level (i.e. the planning committee) rather than the professional planners, and may reflect the same level of insecurity about design and construction techniques in councillors as in the general public.

- *Attitudes towards 'non-traditional' construction* in the industry. There have been many attempts to move away from the traditional 'brick on brick' approach to house building. Factory production of housing is not new. Le Corbusier advocated it in a chapter entitled 'A house is a machine for living in' in his book *Vers un Architecture* (Le Corbusier, 1923/1970). In 1968, the Weir Housing Corporation in Scotland – a private house builder – concluded that using mass-production techniques for mass-produced housing for sale (as in the car industry) was feasible but not acceptable. They said 'What is needed is not a revolution in technology – that is here already – but a revolution in thinking'. Memories of 1960s' and 1970s' factory-produced housing are as painful to the industry as they are to the consumer. And many house builders are content to continue with the old techniques because they do not believe that they would provide either greater consumer choice or lower capital cost. And it might be that they would not have the right skills available nor be willing or able to invest in these skills to use different techniques.

What do consumers want?

Research carried out into consumer satisfaction in housing shows that the vast majority of householders are satisfied with their house. Scottish Homes carried out four Consumer Preference Surveys in the mid-1990s and each of them indicated that around 90 per cent of home-owners were satisfied or highly satisfied with their home. There was no separate analysis for new houses, but it would be unlikely that owners of these houses would be dramatically out of line with the norm.

So what is it that consumers look for? The Scottish Consumer Preference Surveys reinforced the commonly held belief that the three most important factors are location, location and location. Further work recently carried out by MVA Ltd for Scottish Homes, but not published, placed location and price at the top of purchasers' criteria. This study, which was the first part of a larger exercise into 'Improving Understanding of Popular Quality and Design among Home-owners', was carried out through a series of interviews and focus groups in Central Scotland.

The research was conducted with recent house buyers (within 18 months from the survey date) and was confined to the lower end of the house-price market (£30,000–£69,000) – the mass market. The principal purpose of this phase of the study was to investigate the purchase process, and the variables related to quality and design that respondents took into account when choosing a home. Many of the respondents had decided before seeking a house whether they wanted a new one or an old one, based on their own preconceptions or experience of the market. The study therefore gives some indication of consumer attitudes.

The perceived characteristics of new houses were:

- low cost of initial survey

- low maintenance costs

- lower cost of heating

- small rooms, especially bedrooms

- 'box-like', characterless

- houses built close together

- thin walls, poor soundproofing

- poor storage space

- convenience of buying new house with all the fitments at fixed price.

The perceived characteristics of old houses were:

- expensive survey required

- high maintenance cost

- higher costs of heating

- large rooms

- high ceilings

- more 'character'

- solid walls, good soundproofing.

There were a number of key areas in new housing that were important to the respondents:

- *Number of bedrooms*: one of the three most important criteria in buying a house (along with price and location). Many were looking for a three-bedroom house, but the third room was nearly always too small.

- *Size of rooms*: it was felt that bedrooms were often designed to be too small.

- *Soundproofing*: most felt that soundproofing was poor.

- *Storage*: most felt that there was a lack of storage space.

- *Type of heating*: gas central heating was considered to be the most cost-effective. Some respondents chose new houses because they had better insulation and lower ceilings. There was little evidence that energy efficiency was seen as a 'green issue', rather than as a running cost issue.

- *Garden and outdoor privacy*: seen as important to a large number of respondents. It has to be remembered that Scotland has a higher proportion of flats than the rest of the UK.

- *Decor and fitments*: many strongly desired a property that they could move into without making alterations. A few said that they chose to buy a property that required decoration because they preferred to decorate it to their own taste and that properties requiring decoration or improvements were usually cheaper.

One area of consideration that is of particular interest to the current debate was that of construction quality. Respondents often expressed the view that old houses appeared to be much 'better built', particularly in the quality of materials used. It was felt that old houses were much more 'solid' and that new houses tended to be 'kit built', using cheaper materials and concern was expressed that new buildings would not last long. The speed at which new houses (presumably timber frame) were built led respondents to doubt the quality of the workmanship. A quote from a focus group member highlights the concern:

When they were building it *[my house]* I was actually talking to the men over the fence who were building it and was asking them what they were doing. Usually you see the foundations go down and before you know it the houses are built. But these foundations seemed to be taking ages and I asked them and they said that they were making a certain kind of foundation and they had to make sure that everything was fine. So that made me think that they were taking their time and were not throwing them up like some houses that just seem to appear.

There are a number of conclusions that can be made from this study (if it can be accepted as representative):

- Consumers' top priorities are price, location and house size defined by the number of bedrooms.

- Consumers' concerns about key design issues do not seem to influence the design process.

- Consumers generally do not see the need for greater individuality or choice.

- Consumers' perceptions about how a house ought to be built are based on traditional building processes.

Is there a new-build crisis?

If the available evidence shows that there is a high degree of satisfaction with the end product, why do many housing analysts consider that there are problems with the new-build mass-market sector? Is looking at the product and the industry the best way of examining the issue? Could it be that consumers are cautious about dealing with the mass market for reasons that have less to do with the industry and more to do with the psychology and culture of the housing consumer? Here are five possible clues:

1   *It's not so much the product as the location*

Is it really the product about which the consumer is concerned? 'It's a nice house, but I wish it was somewhere else.' Many of the houses that self-procurers build are similar to those built in estates. Is this the lack of choice, or could it be that the product is acceptable and it is the location that matters?

'Location, location, location' is not only a cliché, but remains one of the most important factors in choosing a house. What is it about location that is important and may be influencing the way consumers behave?

Another study currently being carried out for Scottish Homes collects the attitudes of the occupants of a new rented development (albeit part of a mixed-tenure scheme) over a period of time. The question of what is the most important thing about choosing a house produces the answer – neighbours.

Making the decision to buy a new house in a new area involves moving into unknown territory in terms of neighbours. If you buy a house in an established neighbourhood, you can at least get some understanding of who lives in the area, what the schools will be like, what facilities are available and the stability of the area. New estates situated on the edge of town – or even on brownfield sites – demand an act of faith. New Towns have lost some of their glamour over the years – instant communities do not happen. Consumers know that time is required for facilities to appear. And many of the new estates – though not quite New Town size – are large and can have the feel of pioneering. Could it be that there is nervousness about pioneering, or that we now want instant communities, rather than building one up over a period of time? In other words, that moving into a new estate involves taking a risk about neighbours and neighbourhood – and therefore needs to be carefully considered? Many developers seem to recognise this by describing the estates as 'exclusive' – i.e. that you will find your own social class in the estate.

There is a second issue about location – distance, not just from established facilities, but also from transport. Many new estates on the edge of towns are poorly linked to public transport, particularly transport to work. If new estates were planned with better public transport infrastructure would they be more acceptable?

More research is needed to be able to answer these questions. It would be interesting to know whether there are any differences between sales patterns in different estates, and in particular between peripheral estates and infill developments in established communities; further, whether consumers differentiate between developers.

2   It's a huge investment

To say that buying a house is the biggest single investment that anyone will make is another of the house purchase clichés – but it is true for most people. Potential purchasers therefore will be cautious in making the decision, particularly if they are an early investor in an estate. They need to see other people making the investment as well. Then there is the resale value: 'how long do we need to stay before we get our money back if it all goes wrong?' And the volatility of the markets must contribute to the uncertainty.

Added to this is the lack of real information about the whole cost – including the running costs. Few new housing developments provide energy or potential maintenance costs. Do we need a system for new housing similar to new cars which predicts running costs taking into account lifestyles (for example, whether the house is to be occupied all day with heavy use of energy), and predicts insurance as well as mortgage costs. Could houses be independently assessed for running costs?

Many purchasers in the mass-market sector will also be working at the limit of their personal finances; they will need the biggest mortgage they can get. Perhaps more developments should be sold on a shared ownership basis, such as MacTaggart & Mickel provided in the West of Scotland in the 1950s. But most developers appear to want only a short-term relationship with their customers, and may not have sufficient capital to engage in a long-term relationship.

3   I am afraid of being conned

Consumers appear to lack confidence in the building industry. The new-build sector's image has been dented – rightly – by some very poor press. Nearly everybody has a story to tell about bad workmanship, poor advice and adversarial contracting.

There are of course two sides to all of this. The client has to be clear about what he/she wants and realistic about expectations, and the contractor (in this case the developer) has to deliver a product that is accurately described and provides value for money.

Some of the marketing techniques used by the industry do not encourage consumer confidence. Show houses with internal doors removed to create a greater feeling of space and smaller-scale furniture were just two of the techniques identified by Valerie Karn in her years of studying developers' show houses (Karn, 1994). Pressure sales techniques and the lack of information about energy efficiency were other concerns she identified. But, above all, the impression was given of an industry that wanted to get rid not only of the product but also of the customer. There is little attempt by the developer to create a relationship with the purchaser. The consumer looks for a service, not just a product. With only around 10 per cent of all house sales, new house developers are unlikely to expect many repeat sales. As a consumer good, the traditional aim of developing customer loyalty may not apply to this market.

4   I think houses should be built properly

'The Englishman's home is his castle' – a phrase that encapsulates a whole range of attitudes towards the home: strength, security, privacy. These are to be found, we believe, in brick- and stone-built houses. And so, even if the structure of the house is timber frame, we have to wrap it in brick to give the appearance of a solid building that has been hand-crafted. The Americans and Scandinavians seem content with timber frame wrapped with timber. The Japanese have always regarded timber or even plastic as a sensible external finish.

There is a strange contradiction in what we regard as acceptable building processes. We are quite happy to accept plastic downpipes and UPVC windows in our houses, office buildings that come as a kit of parts to be assembled on site and concrete structures that are 'clipped together' for our schools, but these are not acceptable for the structure of our house. Again, is this a deep-rooted psyche problem?

We have had, of course, problems with prefabricated housing in the 1960s and 1970s that have passed into popular folklore and convey that these processes produce problem houses. Changing folklore is always difficult. If prefabrication is to become acceptable to the consumer (as distinct to the industry), there will have to be openness about the processes and advantages demonstrated in terms of flexibility, lower maintenance and above all costs – capital, running costs and resale value. This is not a task for the industry on its own, but requires the support of government (perhaps funding some demonstrations) and the Consumer Councils that can be seen to be independent.

5   I do not know much about modern design and sustainability

Ask any child (and most adults) to draw a house. It will have two storeys, a front door, four windows, a pitched roof and chimneys. How important is it to our psyche that our houses look like this? And is there something in our collective subconscious that makes us want to have houses that look roughly the same, but with small personalisation, like different front doors? Nothing too different!

In the UK, unlike our Scandinavian neighbours, 'good design' is not regarded as part of our mass culture. This is not a subject that features prominently in our school curricula – indeed, nor does housing, despite its importance to independent living, to economic well-being and to sustainability. When faced with housing as a major consumer issue, therefore, the British public is likely to be under-educated. To be a discerning consumer requires a certain amount of knowledge and understanding, and an ability to ask questions with self-assurance. It also requires a wider appreciation of what is possible and the confidence to challenge what is provided. Without confidence in our own design decisions, are we likely to simply fall back on previous periods for our design aesthetic, and thus be willing to buy 'half-timbered, mock Tudor' housing? And do we buy that because that is what everyone is buying?

What does influence our understanding of design and sustainability? The media is the most obvious influence. There are a large number of popular magazines and television programmes about house design. But these have been mainly about interior 'fashion'. Programmes on new house design and sustainable construction have been relegated to the architectural niche slots late at night on Channel 4. And these tend to be about expensive one-off houses, thus giving strength to the myths that 'Good design costs more' or 'Being green costs more'.

There is a further gap in the media. The second most expensive consumer purchase is likely to be a car. Car magazines and newspapers deal not only with the image, but also with the performance of the car. They take manufacturers' new products to bits, analysing their construction. They look abroad for new trends. These independent publications are regarded as the consumer's guide. There is no such equivalent for housing.

A further influence is home exhibitions. Thousands of people visit home exhibitions each year and thousands more spend their weekend looking at show houses, even if they have no intention of buying. Again, these concentrate mainly on the interior decor, while show houses built for exhibitions are again at the top end of the range. In Scandinavia, people go to see modern building designs at affordable levels. There has been a tradition of demonstration homes in the UK that has helped to push forward the public's view of what is possible or desirable. Milton Keynes has mounted a number of demonstration projects, usually as the result of competitions. The latest demonstration project was the 100-house 'Homes of the Future' development, part of Glasgow City of Architecture and Design 1999, which sold extremely quickly as high-density housing. More demonstration homes are needed to help widen the consumer's view of what is possible. (An interesting side comment on the industry, however, is that, when one of the builders involved in 'Homes of the Future' was asked if the experience had changed their board's strategy, they replied no. They thought that there was not a huge demand for this kind of development and that they would continue to develop their landbank with traditional housing! Their landbank is of course mainly in greenfield sites.)

Improving understanding also needs improved information and advice. Where does the first-time buyer go for guidance? In the mid-1990s, the Joseph Rowntree Foundation funded a guide to home buying looking at the product as well as the process (Joseph Rowntree Foundation, 1995). It is not clear what impact that may have had on consumers, but the idea could be revived, maybe as a web site.

In all of this, the aim must be to create an 'intelligent client', not just a consumer of a product.

Conclusion

Consumers appear on the whole to be satisfied with their housing – including the houses provided in the mass-market sector. Evidence of a growing demand for more choice is difficult to come by, but may be indicated by the growth of a wider range of new house providers – albeit at present targeting niche and higher-income households. Location and cost are at the top of consumers' priorities, and they are not well equipped to act as 'intelligent clients'. Their vision needs to be expanded.

The industry has a major part to play in improving its image and in being less conservative about the choices that it makes available. This is not a simple situation, for providing more choice without better information and education would not improve the take-up of new housing. It needs a rethink of both the industry and the attitudes of the British house-buying consumer. The answer to 'location, location, location' may well be 'education, education, education'!

References

Karn, V. (1994) *New Homes in the 1990s: A Study of the Design, Space and Amenities in Housing Association and Private Sector Housing.* York: Joseph Rowntree Foundation

Joseph Rowntree Foundation (1995) *Housing Quality: A Practical Guide for Tenants and their Representatives.* York: Joseph Rowntree Foundation

Le Corbusier (1923/1970) *Towards a New Architecture* ('Vers une Architecture'). London: Architectural Press

6 CONSUMER HOUSING PREFERENCES IN A MARKET CONTEXT

Alan Hooper

Summary

This chapter examines the context within which consumers' housing choices are made in Britain at the present time. The focus is upon owner-occupied housing as the majority tenure, but about which comparatively little is known from the consumers' perspective. The consequences of the interaction of housing market processes with land-use planning policies are traced in terms of the impact on trends in the production of the housing commodity, and in the recomposition of the bundle of attributes that are available for consumption on purchase of a dwelling. Expressed consumer preference for increased provision of space is contrasted with housing and land market trends, and with current fashions in planning policy, both of which interact to significantly constrain the consumption of housing space. The consequences for the new housing product are discussed, together with a perceived polarisation in the residential built environment which mirrors that in housing tenure and income distribution.

Introduction

The study of consumer preferences in relation to housing choice has an uneven history in the United Kingdom, but is closely related to the policy significance of tenure sector change over time. An initial concentration upon the housing preferences of public sector tenants has been replaced since the 1980s with a developing interest in the housing choices of those in the owner-occupied sector, as this sector has become the dominant tenure (with 67 per cent of households nationally at the time of the 1991 Census). This dominance has been achieved comparatively recently, with a rate of increase of 21 per cent from 1969–90 representing the second fastest in Europe over that time period (Radley, 1997). It is somewhat ironic that less is known about housing choice in a market context than in the constrained context of social housing provision, for, in the latter, choice is mediated strongly by housing management practices (Franklin and Clapham, 1997; Somerville and Steele, 1995).

This is not to assert that choice in the private sector is unconstrained, or that it is not mediated through a set of social practices and institutions. It does suggest, however, that what has been termed each 'structure of housing provision' (Ball, 1983) has a historically and socially determined set of institutions through which market forces are filtered. Rather than constituting relatively stable, culturally determined 'housing norms', housing choices are influenced both by the complex bundle of attributes that constitute the housing commodity and by the sets of institutions and structures that constitute the housing market in any given context:

> People do not abstractly demand packaged housing-bundle combinations .... independent of the housing market institutions that provide the direction to that market.
>
> (Shlay, 1987)

This point was also argued in the *Housing Attitudes Survey* (Hedges and Clemens, 1994):

> ... public attitudes are too conditioned by the characteristics of the actual housing market for people to stand back and separate out the intrinsic desirability of ownership as such from the desirability conferred on it by circumstances. Preferences expressed in favour of owning need to be assessed against this background, and should not be regarded as absolutes. A change in the context might lead to a different balance of preferences.

Housing market dynamics, land use regulation and tax policies are some of the important factors that structure residential options so that housing choices are constrained, and thus in many contexts housing choice behaviour may not reflect overall housing desires because these choices come in predictable packages with little flexibility (Shlay, 1985). To a significant extent in the UK, even the provision of social housing is now mediated through a quasi-market context (Malpass, 2000), and hence housing choices and preferences in that structure of provision will differ from those exercised under a predominantly public sector mode of provision as was the case up until the end of the 1970s.

It may be useful, therefore, to briefly review what is known about housing choices and preferences in the private sector, and then to relate these revealed preferences to the set of institutional structures under which they are expressed.

Private sector housing preferences

The housing market

For most of the post-war period, governments, housing market institutions and households have operated in an environment where house price inflation has generally outstripped the general rate of inflation (Forrest *et al.*, 1997; Saunders, 1990). In a context in which dwellings represented appreciating assets, it is not surprising, therefore, to find that home-ownership has consistently been the expressed tenure preference of a majority of respondents to surveys concerned with housing choice (Hedges and Clemens, 1994; Radley, 1997). The *Housing Attitudes Survey* (conducted during the most prolonged post-war slump in the housing market) indicated that, amongst potential movers, there was an indication of a trend even further towards owner-occupation than the 67 per cent recorded at the 1991 Census, with a projection of 70 per cent. A similar conclusion was reached in a study of the limits to increases in owner-occupation:

> At present, despite the severity and the length of downturn in the housing market, most people are still relatively optimistic about house prices and are positive about the attractions of owning a home in the long term.
> (Radley, 1997)

The most recent estimate of the sustainable limit for owner-occupation in 2001 has been put at a maximum of 72 per cent, giving a slack of only 4 per cent above the estimate of 68 per cent for 1997 (Radley, 1997). Hence, the future rate of increase in home-ownership is likely to be much slower than in the past, but it is likely to remain the dominant tenure for the foreseeable future.

Surveys conducted on behalf of the Halifax and New Homes Marketing Board between 1995 and 1998 indicate a clear difference in perceptions between existing owner-occupiers and first-time buyers in relation to the housing market (Mulholland Research Associates, 1995, 1996, 1997). The confidence of first-time buyers in the housing market had clearly been severely affected by the housing market slump of the early 1990s, and particularly by the incidence of negative equity. This finding has been corroborated by other research (Forrest et al., 1997; Radley, 1997). The biggest falls in confidence in the housing market and the relative attractions of owner-occupation between the start and end of the recession occurred amongst the younger age groups (18–24 and 25–34), which had been adversely affected by their relatively recent entry to the housing market and by adverse trends in the employment market. Once again, all sources confirm that attitudes towards owner-occupation changed rapidly with improvements in the housing market: 'More generally, there was no evidence that our home-owners had become disillusioned with owner-occupation'(Forrest et al., 1997). What appears to have developed is an evolution in the UK housing market towards a stage of maturity – many of those groups which had been attracted to home-ownership at an accelerated rate since the 1970s had experienced a wide range of housing market conditions, and those new and aspiring entrants to the sector had endured the first post-war period of significant negative equity. As Forrest et al. (1997) note:

There *is*, however, greater caution, more awareness of the details of mortgage finance and the alternatives on offer and a greater emphasis on the dwelling as a consumption rather than an investment good. And people themselves are more conscious of having *sustainable* levels of housing investment in a more uncertain world.

National house prices between 1997 and 2000 have followed a consistently upward trend, with very high escalation in the London housing market, where annual house price inflation hit a peak of 30 per cent between 1998 and 1999. This rate of house-price change is likely to have had an adverse effect upon first-time buyers in particular, but, since the London housing market is affected by a special set of circumstances, the difficulties for first-time buyers outside the capital are likely to have been less severe, reflecting less violent housing market fluctuations. These house price trends indicate that housing market adjustments had largely removed the problem of negative equity as a structural problem by the end of the 1990s: 'the market has adjusted to take care of the problems of the 1990s without any external intervention' (Forrest *et al.*, 1997). Indeed, the Housing Green Paper *Quality and Choice* (Department of the Environment, Transport and the Regions, 2000a) now proposes special measures to offset the negative consequences for key workers of very high house prices in London.

While annual house price inflation in London hit a peak of 30 per cent in 1988/89 and 1998/99, the number of sales in the last year has remained relatively flat, suggesting that the strong growth of house prices in London is likely to have reflected acute land shortages. Recent research has demonstrated the acute pressure on the housing market in London from both the increase in new household formation and from international migration (Whitehead *et al.*, 1999). But such demographic pressures are mediated by institutional factors. As Cheshire and Sheppard (2000) observe, from 1892 to 1931, despite an increase in the number of households of 61 per cent and substantial real growth in incomes, the real price of land actually fell. The reason is to be found in a relatively competitive market for land, unconstrained by a comprehensive system of land use regulation. With the institution of such a system after 1947 through successive town and country planning acts:

> The constraints we apply via urban containment on the supply of the most basic attribute of housing – space – have been progressively tightened since 1947.
> (Cheshire and Sheppard, 2000)

A corollary is that, from 1947 to 1998, the real price of housing land is estimated to have increased by a factor of 7 or 8 (Cheshire and Sheppard, 2000). Because of supply-side inelasticity exacerbated by the planning system, there is increasing instability in housing markets over the cycle (Ball, 1996; Cheshire and Sheppard, 2000). Notwithstanding this, there are consequences not only for the price of housing, but also for the quantity of housing produced and its characteristics (Bramley et al., 1995).

The housing bundle

Economists characterise housing as a complex bundle of attributes (Maclennan, 1982). Some of these attributes derive from the 'internal' characteristics of the unit as a dwelling providing shelter and living accommodation, whereas others derive from the location of the unit, which provides access to a range of utilities, services and facilities. Each of these attributes contributes to the price of the unit, along with more symbolic aspects. One of the key attributes, which unites the 'internal' and 'external' components, is space, and it is this attribute that is affected in a fundamental, if unintended, manner by the operation of the planning system.

In the short term, the space available to house buyers for purchase is largely determined by the existing stock of housing. Provision of new build in any one year accounts for only 1–2 per cent increase in the available stock. The composition of the existing stock is changing very slowly, with only 4 per cent of dwellings added and 1 per cent lost between 1991 and 1996 (Department of the Environment, Transport and the Regions, 1998). Some 45 per cent of dwellings were built over 50 years ago, and a quarter of the stock dates from before the First World War (Department of the Environment, Transport and the Regions, 1998). At an aggregate level, it has been estimated that the length of time each dwelling would have to last if every completion replaced a unit of existing stock is about five times longer than Japan, 30 per cent longer than France and twice as long as The Netherlands or Germany. This is because the United Kingdom builds relatively little new housing compared to other developed countries (Barlow, 2001).

The new-build supply now has quite specific characteristics. Of dwellings added to the stock between 1991 and 1996, 87 per cent were through new build and 13 per cent through conversions (Department of the Environment, Transport and the Regions, 1998). In 1999, around 168,000 new dwellings were completed, of which 132,000 were built by speculative house builders. This predominance of private sector provision ensures that households face a limited choice in housing tenures or ways in which they can secure a new home (Barlow, 2001).

The *English House Condition Survey*, 1996 (Department of the Environment, Transport and the Regions, 1998), indicates that dwellings in England are predominantly houses – only 19 per cent are flats. Detached houses represent 30 per cent of dwellings built 1991–96, compared to 20 per cent of the stock existing in 1991. The average usable floor area for all dwellings in England is 85 square metres, virtually the same as France and Germany but only half that of the USA. For houses it is 90 square metres and flats 59 square metres. Over time, dwellings added to the stock have become smaller – the average size for a post-1980 dwelling unit is 76 square metres, which is 10 per cent smaller than those built before 1980. Between 1991 and 1996, there was a polarisation in building towards smaller one- and two-bedroom properties, and larger four or more bedroom family houses. However, in the 1990s, whilst the trend in housing production of one- and two-bedroom dwellings was downwards (from 78,304 to 49,693 units per annum, 1990–97), the trend for three- and four-bedroom dwellings was upwards (from 76,271 to 97,647 units, 1990–97). Most houses stand on plots of between 1,000 and 500 square metres. Plot sizes vary by age, type and tenure. Houses built since 1980 have plots, on average, 20 per cent smaller than those built between 1919 and 1964. The relationship between dwelling size, tenure, house price and land price is complex, and varies over time, but its significance was recognised as early as 1973 in the pioneering study of the impact of the British planning system (Hall *et al.*, 1973). The Urban Task Force noted in its report (1999) that the question of whether there is a case for reintroducing some form of minimum space standards in respect of housing should be remitted for further government consideration, but there has been no response to this issue in the Urban White Paper (Department of the Environment, Transport and the Regions, 2000b).

The pressure on residential space standards identified in Hall *et al.*'s classic study is clearly continuing, and data on recent house and plot sizes are consistent with the asserted impacts upon land and house prices found in recent economic analyses (Bramley *et al.*, 1995; Cheshire and Sheppard, 2000). Moreover, it has recently been demonstrated that the relative increases in those housing attributes that can be considered to be in relatively fixed or shrinking supply (such as land and space) compared with those in reproducible supply indicate much more rapid increases in price between 1984 and 1993 for the former. One unintended consequence of this inflation in housing land price is that, as the distribution of income becomes more unequal, the ability of higher-income households to outbid lower-income households for locationally fixed amenities is further strengthened. Thus, the intensified income inequality is translated into more spatial and social segregation (Cheshire and Sheppard, 2000). It is not surprising, therefore, to find that the highest levels of private sector overcrowding are to be found in larger urban areas and of social sector overcrowding in London and the South East (Department of the Environment, Transport and the Regions, 1998).

The new housing product

It has been argued that the rate of change in the type of housing products offered by speculative house builders is exceptionally slow, compared to many other industries (Barlow, 2000). Whereas house builders have moved away from the 1950s' and 1960s' era of mass-produced standardised products, the introduction of 'mass-customised' products through innovation in the construction process has been negligible. Responses have largely been limited to slightly greater degrees of choice by consumers in fixtures and fittings (Nicol and Hooper, 1999), rather than to any real flexibility in design or layout.

One of the main reasons for this conservatism has been the structural context in which the industry operates. Processes of concentration and specialisation, together with the increased volatility in the housing market, have resulted in mounting difficulties for the house-building industry in responding to market signals and in planning its short-term output (Barlow, 2000). Comparing the 1980s and the 1990s, it seems that house price inflation has remained comparatively stable (outside London), whereas land prices have seen sharp upward and downward swings since 1990. There is thus a growing short-term mismatch between land and house inflation, which places additional pressure upon the land-buying activities of house-building companies (Barlow, 2000). This has been exacerbated by the general tightening up of the planning system since the initiation of a 'plan-led' system since the 1990 Town and Country Planning Act, compounded by the introduction of a 'sequential approach' to land release in favour of brownfield housing sites under *Planning Policy Guidance Note 3: Housing* (Department of the Environment, Transport and the Regions, 2000c). One of the few ways to standardise elements of the production process, given the prevailing building technology, has been to rely upon a greater range of standardised house types (Hooper and Nicol, 1999; Nicol and Hooper, 1999). Such house types generally permit only cosmetic changes by customers, and then largely to those units bought 'off-plan' (i.e. in advance of construction), especially under conditions of market downturn. Customers therefore have to look to other aspects of new housing consumption, such as service provision, in order to choose between products or producers (Barlow and Ozaki, 2000). This has to be set against the findings of surveys which indicate that more than 83 per cent of house buyers would like to be offered greater choice over the initial design of their homes, especially in relation to the future adaptability of layout to accommodate change (Barlow and Ozaki, 2000). To date, then, the 'mass customisation' of housing provision has not occurred in the United Kingdom.

It has been concluded that 'there has been little interest in providing more customised housing products in the UK housebuilding industry. Perhaps the foremost inhibitors are the development process itself and the lack of competition from alternative suppliers. The dominant competitive strategy of the speculative housebuilding industry has largely been influenced by the value of land and profits accruing from returns of land development' (Barlow and Ozaki, 2000), rather than from product or process innovation. This is not to argue that the house-building industry has ignored an increased awareness of customer preferences, but rather to indicate that, to date, its response has been to improve customer care rather than to develop customisation in the product process.

Customers and new housing

The industry's own surveys tend to show a high level of satisfaction with its current products (Dunmore, quoted in Barlow and Ozaki, 2000; Mulholland Research Associates, 1995), with the great majority of respondents willing to buy another new home in the future, particularly amongst upper-income groups. The comparative preferences for new dwellings and existing stock vary with the condition of the housing market (Mulholland Research Associates, 1996, 1997) – among other factors – and there are significant differences between first-time buyers and existing owner-occupiers, which again vary over time.

Whilst a majority of surveyed owners in 1995 considered that the size of their house and their garden was adequate, 12 per cent considered that their homes were too small and 12 per cent considered that their gardens were too small (Mulholland

Research Associates, 1995). In 1997, the second major complaint about brand new homes (after 'value for money' problems) was recorded as 'lack of space' factors (particularly relating to bedrooms) (Mulholland Research Associates, 1997), and the 'value for money' problems also included a strong preference for additional space in new homes. Interestingly, the survey recorded a perception that more could be done to improve internal design and construction through innovation, though the suggestions offered by consumers related more to problems with site density and spaciousness of homes than to any particularly new ideas (Mulholland Research Associates, 1997). Volume house-building companies conduct their own surveys of customer satisfaction, both in relation to the sales process and 'customer care'. These contribute to an interactive process of design modification which is consumer influenced but not consumer led (Hooper, 1999; Hooper and Nicol, 2000).

It is relevant to note at this juncture that the *Housing Attitudes Survey* found that, when it comes to improving their present situation, householders are more likely to give priority to the accommodation itself over the area or location. The researchers conclude that regarding the house as having more scope for improvement than the area is an attitude linked – though mostly not very strongly – to correlates of area quality such as the owner-occupied percentage and population density. In terms of housing factors, dwelling type appears to be an important variable in satisfaction levels. There is a substantial difference between respondents in flats and those in houses, the latter rating their areas a good deal better. Moreover, within the spectrum of houses, there is a marked progression in area satisfaction from terraced houses to semis to detached (Hedges and Clemens, 1994). Furthermore, population density shows a marked inverse relationship between density and satisfaction.

In relation to questions addressed specifically to space in the home, the *Housing Attitudes Survey* indicated that 72 per cent of the sample were satisfied with the number of rooms they had, whereas 22 per cent said they had too few and 6 per cent too many rooms. No fewer than 46 per cent felt that at least one of their rooms was too small. Overall, the researchers found there was a generalised rather than a very discriminatory desire for more space, but many households felt there was a shortage of space.

In terms of dwelling type, of those likely to move, the *Housing Attitudes Survey* found that 83 per cent preferred houses and 8 per cent flats.

In their study of home-owners on new estates, Forrest *et al.* (1997) found similar results. Overall, 89 per cent of respondents said they were either very satisfied (48 per cent) or fairly satisfied (41 per cent) with their home, and only 6 per cent expressed some degree of dissatisfaction. As the researchers note, this is similar to the findings of the *Housing in England 1994/95 Survey* (ONS, 1996). Again, whereas the majority of households (65 per cent) felt that they had an adequate number of rooms, a significant minority (33 per cent) had too few rooms. Forrest *et al.* found a higher level of dissatisfaction with the size of various rooms compared with the *Housing in England 1994/95 Survey*, and dissatisfaction with the dwelling, where it occurred, centred around room sizes and the number of rooms available.

There thus appears to be an accumulating body of evidence that housing consumers are experiencing a growing pressure on the amount of domestic space that they can buy throughout the housing market and that, in general, space is the most valued criterion for all household types. Space is high on the list of priorities of the increasing number of one-person households, and many such households seek to gain the maximum space they can afford (Hooper *et al.*, 1998). Not surprisingly, this pressure is especially evident in the South East, and particularly in London. Nor is this issue one that can be simply addressed through technological innovation in the building process or through design. Indeed, initial evaluations of the Millennium Home in the Integer programme indicated that spaciousness in a dwelling is not necessarily synonymous with consumer preferences for designed space (Haddon, 1998). Hanson has observed a preference amongst both housing producers and consumers in the private sector for maximising the number of rooms for any given house space configuration (Hanson, 1999), and this too may be partly explained by housing market pressures, mediated by the land-use planning system.

Conclusions

It seems clear that comparatively little is known in depth about the housing preferences of owner-occupiers in general, and the occupiers of newly built housing in particular. What is known seems to reflect a generally conservative stance with respect to housing attributes, but this is perhaps unsurprising given the recent and existing structural context in which the market for owner-occupied dwellings has developed. Overwhelmingly, the major reason for consumer choice of housing relates to its perceived utility – whereas appearance can be an important reason for rejecting a particular house, it is not usually a major reason for choosing to acquire it (Angle and Malam, 1998). Apart from location, space seems to be a major factor for most groups in their choice of housing in the private market. Yet space inside the home appears to be one of the least important factors to be considered by those who regulate housing production, at least since the abandonment of Parker Morris standards. The impact upon both private and social housing sectors has been readily discernible (Karn and Sheridan, 1994). Apart from the Building

Regulations and the National House Building Council Standards, there is remarkably little regulation of domestic space standards.

Whilst the planning system does not regulate domestic space standards directly (except through daylight and sunlight considerations, and upon minimum garden sizes, where these apply), the indirect effect upon declining housing space seems apparent. This has implications both for housing consumers and urban design (Urban Task Force, 1999). This effect is, however, mediated by the housing market and, consequently, its effects are most apparent where the housing market is particularly constrained. Given that the effects of the planning system are subject to significant time lags – not least because of the 'implementation gap' that existed in the planning system prior to the establishment of the 'plan-led' system in 1990 (Bramley *et al.*, 1995) – the housing market and land markets do not necessarily share short-term trends. As a result, the 'lumpiness' of land release that characterises the present system of land supply for housing can easily exacerbate housing market pressures and amplify the already increasingly volatile housing market. To the extent that a 'plan, monitor and manage' approach will replace a 'predict and provide' framework, that approach (and its corollary, the sequential approach to brownfield land release) is likely to lead to a continued general constraint in high-demand areas and a 'lumpiness' in land supply for housing. Indeed, the new 'call-in' powers relating to housing developments of over 150 units on greenfield land announced in 2000 are likely to exacerbate the general overall speed of response of the planning system in relation to planning permission for residential development, which is already a major criticism made by the house-building industry.

The overall tenor of both the Urban Task Force Report (1999) and the Urban White Paper (Department of the Environment,

Transport and the Regions, 2000b) is to encourage an increase in density of residential development, from the average 25 dwellings per hectare of new development of the present to 30–50 dwellings per hectare, with increased densities in major urban centres, a measure put into effect by recent planning guidance (Department of the Environment, Transport and the Regions, 2000c). This measure is likely to further exacerbate the pressure on domestic space in terms of size of average dwelling and plot size. At the upper end of the housing market, as real incomes continue to increase we are likely to find:

- continued urban exodus to suburban and ex-urban locations to maximise space consumption within existing constraints and/or an increase in second-home ownership

- within urban areas, the erection of new large dwellings on increasingly small plots and the extension of existing dwellings to the limits of the plot capacity

- the progressive intensification of existing suburban development through infilling and redevelopment – the 'town-cramming' debate will be essentially suburban in focus.

At the lower end of the market, land constraints will be likely to:

- lead to increased densities in housing layouts by house-building companies to offset increased land costs and reduction in supply of urban land, with consequent adverse impacts upon both plot size and general residential amenity and domestic space

- encourage reduced storage provision (exacerbated by the trend to discourage the provision of garages)

- further discourage the provision of one- and two-bedroom dwellings (compounded by current changes to the Building Regulations in relation to accessibility requirements).

The overall effect, notwithstanding the hopes of the Urban White Paper to eradicate the segregation of urban space based upon housing tenure, will be to ossify the existing tenure structure exhibited in the housing market and to exaggerate patterns of social differentiation which have their basis in the operation of the housing system.

To the extent that these trends have their basis in the land market, their continued and even exacerbated operation will continue to frustrate attempts to effect a step-change in technological innovation in the housing production process, reinforcing the regressive outcomes currently evident in the operation of the housing market and buttressing the traditional relationship between housing producers and consumers in the UK.

References

Angle, H. and Malam, S. (1998) *Kerb Appeal*. Winchester: Popular Housing Forum (now Popular Housing Group)

Ball, M. (1983) *Housing Policy and Economic Power: The Political Economy of Owner Occupation*. London: Methuen

Ball, M. (1996) *Housing and Construction: A Troubled Relationship?* Bristol: The Policy Press

Barlow, J. (2000) *Private Sector Housebuilding: Structure and Strategies into the 21st Century*. London: Council of Mortgage Lenders

Barlow, J. (2001) *Land for Housing*. York: YPS for the Joseph Rowntree Foundation

Barlow, J. and Ozaki, R. (2000) 'User needs, customisation and new technology in UK house building', paper presented at the EHNR 2000 conference, Gävle, Sweden, 26–30 June

Bramley, G., Bartlett, W. and Lambert, C. (1995) *Planning, the Market and Private Housebuilding*. London: UCL Press

Cheshire, P. and Sheppard, S. (2000) 'Building on brown fields: the long term price we pay', *Planning in London*, Vol. 33, pp. 34–6

Department of the Environment, Transport and the Regions (DETR) (1998) *English House Condition Survey, 1996*. London: DETR

Department of the Environment, Transport and the Regions (DETR) (2000a) *Quality and Choice – a Decent Home for all – the Housing Green Paper*. London: HMSO

Department of the Environment, Transport and the Regions (DETR) (2000b) *Our Towns and Cities: The Future: Delivering an Urban Renaissance*. Cm. 4911. London: HMSO

Department of the Environment, Transport and the Regions (DETR) (2000c) *Planning Policy Guidance Note 3: Housing*. London: The Stationery Office

Forrest, R., Kennet, T. and Leather, P. (1997) *Homeowners on New Estates in the 1990s*. Bristol: The Policy Press

Franklin, B. and Clapham, D. (1997) 'The social construction of housing management', *Housing Studies*, Vol. 12, No. 1, pp. 7–12

Haddon, L. (1998) 'Consumer research and tenant consultation: a report on Phase 2 of the INTEGER Programme', mimeo

Hall, P., Gracey, H., Drewett, R. and Thomas, R. (1973) *The Containment of Urban England* (2 vols). London: George Allen & Unwin

Hanson, J. (1999) *Decoding Homes and Houses*. Cambridge: Cambridge University Press

Hedges, B. and Clemens, S. (1994) *Housing Attitudes Survey*. London: HMSO

Hooper, A. (1999) *Design for Living: Constructing the Residential Built Environment in the 21st Century*. London: Town and Country Planning Association

Hooper, A. and Nicol, C. (1999) 'The design and planning of residential development: standard house types in the speculative housebuilding industry', *Environment and Planning B: Planning and Design*, Vol. 26, pp. 793–805

Hooper, A. and Nicol, C. (2000) 'Design practice and volume production in speculative housebuilding', *Construction and Management*, Vol. 18, pp. 295–310

Hooper, A., Dunmore, K. and Hughes, M. (1998) *Home Alone: The Housing Preferences of One-person Households*. Amersham: National House Building Council

Karn, V. and Sheridan, L. (1994) *New Homes in the 1990s: A Study of Design, Space and Amenity in Housing Association and Private Sector Production*. York: Joseph Rowntree Foundation

Maclennan, D. (1982) *Housing Economics: An Applied Approach*. Harlow: Longman

Malpass, P. (2000) *Housing Associations and Housing Policy*. London: Macmillan

Mulholland Research Associates Ltd (1995) *Brand New Home Owner Attitude Survey*. London: New Homes Marketing Board

Mulholland Research Associates Ltd (1996) *Consumer Confidence in the Housing Market*. London: Halifax/New Homes Marketing Board

Mulholland Research Associates Ltd (1997) *Report of Research Findings on the Housing Market: Consumer Confidence, Product and Location Requirements*. London: Halifax/HouseBuilders Federation

Nicol, C. and Hooper, A. (1999) 'Contemporary change and the housebuilding industry: concentration and standardisation', *Housing Studies*, Vol. 14, No. 1, pp. 57–76

Office of National Statistics (1996) *Housing in England 1994/95 Survey*. London: HMSO

Radley, S. (1997) *Sustainable Home Ownership: A New Concept*. York: Joseph Rowntree Foundation

Saunders, P. (1990) *A Nation of Homeowners*. London: Unwin Hyman

Shlay, A.B. (1985) 'Castles in the sky: measuring housing and neighbourhood ideology', *Environment and Behavior*, Vol. 17, No. 5, pp. 593–626

Shlay, A.B. (1987) 'Who governs housing preferences? Comment on Morris', *Environment and Behavior*, Vol. 19, No. 1, pp. 121–36

Somerville, P. and Steele, A. (1995) 'Making sense of tenant participation', *Netherlands Journal of Housing and the Built Environment*, Vol. 10, No. 3, pp. 259–81

Urban Task Force (1999) *Towards an Urban Renaissance*. London: E. & F.N. Spon

Whitehead, C., Holmans, A., Marshall, D., Porter C. and Gordon, I.(1999) *Housing Need in the South East*. Discussion Paper 112. Cambridge: Department of Land Economy, University of Cambridge